SAYING ONE THING, MEANING ANOTHER:

ACTIVITIES FOR CLARIFYING AMBIGUOUS LANGUAGE

CECILE CYRUL SPECTOR, PH.D.

SUPER DUPER® PUBLICATIONS
GREENVILLE, SOUTH CAROLINA

© 1997 by Cecile Cyrul Spector

Cecile Cyrul Spector grants limited rights to individual professionals to reproduce and distribute pages that indicate duplication is permissible. Pages can be used for instruction only and must include Cecile Cyrul Spector's copyright notice. All rights are reserved for pages without the permission-to-reprint notice. No part of these pages may be reproduced in any form, electronic or mechanical, including photocopy, recording, or any information storage and retrieval system without permission in writing from the author.

Library of Congress Cataloging-in-Publication Data

Spector, Cecile Cyrul
    Saying one thing, meaning another : activities for clarifying ambiguous language / Cecile Cyrul Spector ; [illustrations by Patti Argoff].
         p.   cm.
    Includes bibliographical references (p.).
    ISBN 1-888222-10-7 (pbk.)
    1. Ambiguity.   I. Title.
P299.A46S64   1997
401'.4—dc21   97-34322
                                                                                                       CIP

08 07 06 05 04   9 8 7 6 5

Illustrations by Patti Argoff

Printed in the United States of America

Super Duper® Publications
Post Office Box 24997, Greenville, South Carolina 29616
www.superduperinc.com • 1-800-277-8737 • Fax 1-800-978-7379
customerhelp@superduperinc.com

DEDICATION

For Mort, my husband and best friend.

It had to be you.

TABLE OF CONTENTS

PREFACE ix

CHAPTER 1
AMBIGUOUS LANGUAGE: AN OVERVIEW 1
    Purpose of this Resource 1
    The Pervasiveness of Ambiguities in Everyday Language ... 2
    Problems Caused by Poor Understanding 7
    Populations Who Can Benefit from
    Saying One Thing, Meaning Another 9
    The Influence of Cognitive Learning Theories 11
    "Meta" Skills and Developing Communicative Competence ... 13
    Skills Needed to Understand and Use Ambiguous Language ... 14
    World Knowledge and Understanding Ambiguity 17
    Learning Ambiguous Material 21

CHAPTER 2
PREINTERVENTION AND INTERVENTION CONSIDERATIONS 25
    Types of Ambiguity Addressed in
    Saying One Thing, Meaning Another 25
    Rationale for Selecting and Presenting Intervention Materials ... 25
    About Context Clues 27
    Using Explanation Tasks to Analyze Ambiguous Language ... 29
    Assessing Understanding of Ambiguities 30
    Developing Individualized Educational Programs (IEPs) ... 30
    Presenting the Intervention Activities 31
    Other Resources That Contain Ambiguous Material 34

CHAPTER 3
WORDS WITH MULTIPLE MEANINGS 35
    Using Context Clues to Determine Word Meaning 37
    Using Context Clues: *Run* 38
    Using Context Clues: *Slip* 40
    Multiple Meanings in Written Paragraphs 42
    Highlighted Homographs 43
    Homographs 47
    Homographs I 48
    Homographs II 51
    Homographs III 55
    Story Paragraph Containing Homographs 58
    Words and Their Meanings 59
    Highlighted Homophones 60

Highlighted Word Story 65
Homophones 66
Homophones I 67
Homophones II 71
Homophones III 75
Additional Activities. 78
Chapter 3 Answer Key 79

CHAPTER 4
DUAL-MEANING SENTENCES 93
Dual-Meaning Sentences 96
Dual-Meaning Sentences I. 97
Dual-Meaning Sentences II 101
Dual-Meaning Sentences III 106
Dual-Meaning Sentences: Indirect and Polite Requests 109
Dual-Meaning Sentences: Polite Evasions 112
Dual-Meaning Sentences: Ironic Utterances. 114
Dual-Meaning Sentences: Sarcastic Utterances 117
Additional Activities. 121
Chapter 4 Answer Key 122

CHAPTER 5
MULTIPLE MEANING PHRASES 131
Highlighted Idioms. 135
Paragraph with Multiple Meaning Words and Phrases 140
Paragraphs from a Teen Magazine. 141
Idioms 142
Idioms I 143
Idioms II 147
Idioms III 151
Idioms IV 156
Matching Individuals with the Appropriate "Compliments" 161
Idioms and Proverbs from Other Countries 162
Idioms That Mean the Same Thing 163
Idioms and Proverbs with Opposite Meanings 164
Idioms with Only a Figurative Meaning 166
Fixed-Order Idioms 168
More Fixed-Order Idioms. 169
Idioms and Phrases with Three Words in Fixed Order 171
Fixed-Order Idiom Definitions I 172

Fixed-Order Idiom Definitions II 174
Fixed-Order Idiom Definitions III 176
Fixed-Order Idiom Definitions IV 178
Fixed-Order Idiom Definitions V 180
Multiple Meaning Phrase Drawings 182
Multiple Meaning Phrase Drawings I 183
Multiple Meaning Phrase Drawings II 185
Additional Activities... 187
Chapter 5 Answer Key 188

CHAPTER 6
AMBIGUITY CAUSED BY CHANGES
IN STRESS AND/OR JUNCTURE 201

Using Stress to Determine Sentence Meaning 203
Stress and/or Juncture 205
Stress and/or Juncture I 206
Stress and/or Juncture II 210
Books You Won't Find at the Library 215
"Knock-Knock" Jokes 217
Creating "Knock-Knock" Jokes 220
Additional Activities.. 223
Chapter 6 Answer Key 224

CHAPTER 7
CLARIFYING AMBIGUOUS UTTERANCES 229

Restating Ambiguous Comments 231
Determining Information Needed to Clarify Ambiguity 235
Additional Activities 239
Chapter 7 Answer Key 240

GLOSSARY 243

APPENDICES 245

A: Populations Who Can Benefit from
   Saying One Thing, Meaning Another 245
B: The Influence of Cognitive Learning Theories 254
C: Suggestions for IEP Goals and Objectives 257
D: Idiom and Proverb Dictionaries and Thesaurus............... 260

REFERENCES 261

PREFACE

When I was six years old, I had a sudden insight: *The same words can mean different things, and the same meaning can be expressed with different words.* I had just moved from Brooklyn, New York, to Columbia, South Carolina. My family and I were invited to visit with our new next-door neighbors, the Withers. During our visit, Mrs. Withers said to her daughter, "Betty Jean, tote the sack a' suckers in here." I was intrigued. What on earth was Mrs. Withers saying? Why couldn't I understand her? She was speaking in English. Well, Betty Jean arrived several moments later carrying a bag filled with lollipops, and the mystery was solved.

My family moved frequently during my childhood, and I was exposed to the speech and language patterns of many different areas. "Soda" was "pop," and "Come and see us soon" was not really an invitation, but merely a polite good-bye. So much to learn!

I'm still intrigued with language that appears to be saying one thing but means another, such as the sign that reads, "Please Go Away!" on the door of a travel agency. Playing with the ambiguities of language can be a pleasant pastime. Imagine, then, the frustration of being unable to "get it" when someone tells a joke, makes a pun, or makes a comment based on double-entendre. One of the ramifications of not understanding ambiguous material is the loss of pleasure found in the many forms of humor and wordplay based on linguistic ambiguity. More important consequences, however, are the detrimental effects it can have on understanding academic materials and interacting in social situations.

Ambiguous utterances are found frequently in our everyday lives. We hear them in conversations, on television and radio, in jokes and riddles, in the movies, and on the Internet. We see ambiguities in advertisements, greeting cards, comic strips, cartoons, and even in textbooks, as well as on tee shirts, store signs, and bumper stickers. In classroom lectures and discussion, teachers and students use many verbal ambiguities. The pervasiveness of ambiguity in everyday life necessitates that we have the ability to interpret such items.

The activities provided in this book are designed to teach comprehension of ambiguous language by making use of a cognitive strategies approach. The research literature indicates that many individuals do not make effective use of their cognitive resources (Buttrill, Niiwaza, Biemer, Takakashi, and Hearn, 1989; Kamhi, 1987; Pehrsson and Denner, 1988; Schumaker, Deshler, Alley, and Warner, 1983; Seidenberg, 1988). They do not know how or when to use task-specific cognitive strategies. However, when such individuals are made aware of the proper strategy to use for a particular task, many of them have then shown that they can use it effectively. Facilitators, such as speech-language pathologists, teachers of students in regular classroom settings, teachers of ESL students, teachers of students with language-learning disorders, and teachers of students with impaired hearing, are needed to help individuals put this approach into practice. The goals of a cognitive strategies approach are to (1) improve the individual's awareness of different types of ambiguity, (2) help the individual find the proper strategy to deal with each type of ambiguity, (3) describe the strategy, and (4) help the individual apply the strategy in appropriate practice materials.

In addition to making use of a cognitive strategies approach, the materials in *Saying One Thing, Meaning Another* were designed to present ambiguous language with a greater degree of contextual support than is generally found for naturally occurring ambiguities, and to provide, in a systematic way, broad exposure to the types of ambiguities that occur frequently in our everyday lives. Once individuals become aware of how to locate and interpret ambiguities, they can apply the strategies they've learned to the understanding and enjoyment of ambiguous material beyond the items found in this book.

Chapter 1 of *Saying One Thing, Meaning Another* provides information about the many factors that affect our skill in understanding ambiguities. It begins with a discussion of the pervasiveness of ambiguities in our everyday lives, and the problems caused by poor understanding of ambiguous material. Next it discusses the diverse populations that can benefit from improved understanding of ambiguous language, including normally achieving individuals; individuals who have language-learning disorders; individuals who have impaired hearing; individuals who have incurred brain injury through trauma, stroke, or other neurological impairments; individuals who are learning English as a second language; and individuals from other culturally and linguistically diverse groups. Chapter 1 also presents principles of cognitive learning theories that provide the basis for the cognitive strategies approach used in this book, as well as the types of skills involved in grasping ambiguities. The various aspects of world knowledge as they impact our understanding of ambiguous material are also considered, as well as the role played by contextual support and frequency of appropriate exposure in enhancing the understanding of ambiguous material.

The intervention component of *Saying One Thing, Meaning Another* provides stimulus materials with specific, detailed directions for examining the different types of ambiguities. Numerous opportunities are offered to probe, explore, and analyze ambiguities that are embedded in appealing and highly motivational materials (for example, jokes, riddles, advertisements, cartoons, comic strips, and bumper stickers). Chapter 2 includes preintervention considerations and information about the intervention activities. Chapter 3 deals with words with more than one meaning, both homographs and homophones. Chapter 4 addresses sentences that can be taken in two ways. Included in this type of ambiguity are sentences that are rendered ambiguous because of a speaker's intention (for example, indirect requests or sarcastic comments). Chapter 5 focuses on analyzing phrases with multiple meanings. The major emphasis is on idiomatic expressions because they occur so frequently in everyday contexts. Chapter 6 addresses the use of changes in stress and/or juncture to change meaning. Finally, Chapter 7 deals with clarifying utterances made ambiguous by poor presupposition, inferencing, and paraphrasing skills. Additional activities are suggested to improve awareness of a speaker's intentions, purposes, and goals.

The facilitator's ongoing verbal mediation is crucial to the process of learning to decipher ambiguities. My experience with children as young as eight years of age, and with adolescents and adults, has shown this to be true. Although some ambiguities may remain elusive, an individual's overall skill in understanding the four types of ambiguity that are emphasized in this resource can be greatly improved.

I owe a debt of gratitude to those who have helped me in preparing this book. First of all, Nancy McKinley, my editor, has always provided suggestions, guidance, and all-around support in the nicest and most patient manner possible. Thanks also to Linda Schreiber and Julie Poquette, who took part in the editing process; Kris Madsen, for her creative handling of the cover design and the book's graphics; Patti Argoff, who created cartoons from my verbal descriptions; and Ruth Arnold, Jean Hamersky, Vicki Lord Larson, Nancy Lund, Karen Middleswarth, Beverly Stene, and Pam Watkins, whose suggestions helped me to improve the organization and presentation of the intervention activities. Gathering suitable humor materials is a time-consuming task. My thanks to Gene Morrissey for his many years of scanning and collecting cartoons for me.

Most of all, I am grateful to my family, who have always wrapped me in a cocoon of love from which I emerge with wings of inspiration: my husband, Mort, who made sure my computer remained "user friendly" and who was always on the alert for stimulus materials; my daughter Lauren and her husband, Richard; my son, Jeff; my daughter Suzanne and her husband, Tommy; my grandchildren, David, Rachel, Sarah, and Stephanie; and, of course, my sister Glady. I love you all dearly.

1

AMBIGUOUS LANGUAGE: AN OVERVIEW

Ambiguous—capable of being understood in two or more possible senses, doubtful, uncertain, obscure

PURPOSE OF THIS RESOURCE

Saying One Thing, Meaning Another: Activities for Clarifying Ambiguous Language was written to provide facilitators with the background information and materials necessary to help individuals, age 10 through adulthood, who need to improve their understanding and use of ambiguous language. Facilitators might include speech-language pathologists, special educators, teachers of ESL, teachers of the hearing impaired, and teachers who work with normally achieving students. This book uses a cognitive strategies approach to address deficits in the comprehension of ambiguities that occur in the following contexts:

- multiple meaning words;
- sentences with two meanings, including indirect or polite requests, polite evasions, and ironic and sarcastic utterances;
- multiple meaning phrases (mainly idioms); and
- changes in stress and/or juncture.

Instructional materials for each of these contexts are provided in Chapters 3 through 6. In addition, Chapter 7 provides material to assist an individual in asking for, and providing, clarifying information when ambiguous comments are made.

Saying One Thing, Meaning Another fosters the development of skills needed to improve mastery of ambiguous items. The support and guidance provided by the facilitator is an essential part of this developmental process. Using the materials in this book, the facilitator can provide the following:

- frequent, structured exposure to the types of ambiguities found in the individual's environment;
- an abundance of appropriate, varying ambiguous materials;
- placement of ambiguities in highly supportive contexts;
- opportunities to obtain an increased world knowledge base;
- assistance in the development of cognitive strategies;
- assistance in making full use of visual and auditory cues; and
- ongoing, interactive discourse during the intervention process.

The background information provided in the remainder of this introduction enables facilitators to review and to consider, on a conscious level, what may already be known about ambiguous language on a subconscious or instinctive level.

THE PERVASIVENESS OF AMBIGUITIES IN EVERYDAY LANGUAGE

ELEMENTS OF AMBIGUITY

There are a great many words, phrases, and sentences in the English language that can be understood in two or more possible senses. One's ability to determine the appropriate interpretation of these linguistic ambiguities is affected by many factors such as context, familiarity, or whether the material is oral or written. The word *fair*, for example, can be used in numerous ways. The weather can be *fair*, a person can have a *fair* complexion, a carnival is sometimes called a *fair*, a passing grade is just *fair*, and treating members of one group the same as members of another is the *fair* thing to do.

Sometimes the spelling of a word helps us to determine its meaning, but not always. *Fair* and *fare* are spelled differently, but just as *fair* can be interpreted in many ways, so can *fare*. Gourmet *fare* can be served at a dinner party, riders pay a *fare* to take the bus, and, people don't always *fare* well at interviews.

Comments such as "John was upset because he spilled the beans" can be understood in two ways. It can be taken literally to mean he dropped a bag of beans all over the floor, or figuratively to mean he inadvertently told a secret.

A simple sentence such as "John loves Marsha" can be stressed in different ways to change the message it imparts. For example, consider "John *loves* Marsha" (I thought he just liked her) or "John loves *Marsha*" (I thought he loved Sue).

A comment such as "Joe ran his hand through his hair and pulled out a cigar" is open to dual interpretations. Did Joe run his hand through his hair and then pull a cigar out of his pocket, or did he pull a cigar out of his hair?

At times, clarity of expression is sacrificed to maintain the natural flow of conversational language. As a consequence, many utterances become ambiguous. For example, use of *he, she, it, they,* or other pronouns in place of a word with a specific referent (such as a proper noun) may prove to be ambiguous and confuse the listener. Consider this sentence: "Suzanne played with the cat while she was eating dinner." Who was eating dinner, Suzanne or the cat? Unless the context in which this utterance was made is known, it is not possible to be sure of the appropriate interpretation. However, to say "Suzanne played with the cat while Suzanne was eating dinner" seems stilted and redundant. (Of course, the wording of this utterance could be changed to eliminate any chance of being misinterpreted: "Suzanne, while eating dinner, played with the cat.")

Indirect requests also can be a source of ambiguity and are frequently misinterpreted. "That piano playing is giving me a headache" appears to be a straightforward comment, but it is really ambiguous because the words do not state the intended meaning, which is "Stop playing the piano." Polite requests often are stated as questions. A telephone caller who asks, "Is your father home?" really means "Let me speak to your father." "Could you hand me that hammer?" is not really a question of one's physical ability, it is a polite way of saying, "Hand me that hammer." In some instances, listeners need to know why the individual made the comment if they are to interpret it correctly. A simple statement such as "It's cool in here" may be an indirect way of saying "Get me a sweater" or "Turn up the heat." Or, it may mean just the opposite: "Look, I've found a place to escape from this terrible heat wave."

Polite evasions are yet another source of ambiguity. When we do not wish to offend someone who has asked a question that is difficult to answer honestly, we will devise a tactful but ambiguous response. For example, when someone asks, "How did you like my brother in the show last night?," a polite but ambiguous response would be, "He certainly can project his voice."

Sarcastic utterances (remarks that are cutting, hostile, or contemptuous) also are ambiguous because they say one thing but mean another. Sarcastic utterances are based on the assumption that the recipient of such a remark will realize that the intended interpretation of the utterance is the opposite of the words stated. Generally, the tone of voice conveys the intention. For example, a girl says to her rather disheveled sibling, "Don't you look marvelous today." Ironic comments also are ambiguous because, like sarcasm, such comments state the opposite of what is believed. Like sarcasm, some ironic comments may be caustic and hurtful, but unlike sarcasm, they also may be gently teasing or humorous (for example, "Isn't it wonderful that it always rains on the weekend when we don't have to work?").

The vernacular of a particular ethnic group, the idiosyncratic speech of individuals from a different geographic area, and language specific to an age, professional, or occupational group may be additional sources of ambiguous language. Conversational remarks made within these groups may be obscure to the outsider. The expression "Don't diss me" (meaning "Don't be disrespectful to me"), for example, is more likely to be used by teenagers than adults.

Words or phrases may become ambiguous without the visual support offered by written text. Spelling often provides clarifying information and helps support the appropriate interpretation. Consider, for example, "He had a pair" and "He had a pear," or "It was just a little wine" and "It was just a little whine." Punctuation, which helps to indicate stress, intonation, and juncture, also helps to provide information necessary for proper interpretation of a potentially ambiguous utterance. For example, major differences in meaning can be caused by adding a comma ("Let's eat Grandma" versus "Let's eat, Grandma") or by changing the placement of a comma ("Lawyers, give poor free legal advice" versus "Lawyers give poor, free legal advice").

Poor presuppositional skills are yet another reason why utterances become ambiguous. Speakers often wrongly assume that the listener already has knowledge of the details in a topic being introduced. This occurs frequently in the conversation of young children. For example, a four-year-old child asks, "Did you ever go to that store? You know, the one near the big tree." She assumes the listener knows the store and the tree to which she is referring. As children develop, so do their presupposition skills. They become more and more aware of what the listener needs to be told if the discourse is to be unambiguous. Unfortunately, some children and even some adults continue to have faulty presuppositional skills and wrongly assume that the listener has the background knowledge essential for understanding a particular topic of conversation. At a social gathering I attended, a young woman stormed into the room and shouted, "I hate when he talks to me that way!" The other guests, not having been privy to the preceding conversation between the young woman and her conversational partner, were left in the dark. Who is "he" and how did he speak to her?

We presuppose by determining what is likely to have come before a particular statement was made. Just as listeners need to know what happened before a statement was made, they also must be able to use inferencing skills to determine the logical consequences of the statement. Inferencing skills affect the way many utterances, such as indirect or polite requests, polite evasions, and sarcastic comments, are interpreted. If the listener cannot infer what the speaker intends to communicate, then the message becomes ambiguous.

Faulty sending or receiving of a verbal utterance also can create ambiguity. Consider the "telephone" game, in which a message is whispered from one person to another and the last person is asked to repeat the first person's utterance. The original utterance in the game is generally a simple, unambiguous statement that becomes more and more obscure, or ambiguous, as the message is received and interpreted based on each person's own fund of knowledge and memory constraints and then verbalized by one person after another. In other words, ambiguity can be created where there is none simply by virtue of a listener hearing a message as shaped by his or her own prior experiences and world knowledge. Of course, hearing impairment also can cause faulty reception of an utterance.

Factors that relate to world knowledge often cause a message, written or verbal, to be ambiguous. Determining what information is relevant about the speaker, the linguistic and physical environment, the social occasion, the purpose of the interaction, and other affective variables influences one's skill in selecting the correct interpretation in a potentially ambiguous utterance. These factors are discussed at length in a latter part of this chapter. Table 1 presents a summary of the elements of ambiguity.

Table 1

ELEMENTS OF AMBIGUITY

LINGUISTIC ELEMENTS

- multiple meaning words
- sentences with dual meanings, including the following:
  - indirect requests
  - polite requests
  - polite evasions
  - ironic and sarcastic utterances
- idiomatic expressions
- changes in sentence stress and/or juncture

CULTURAL ELEMENTS

- lack of familiarity with vernacular of:
  - ethnic group
  - age group
  - professional or occupational group
  - geographic area

PRAGMATIC AND COGNITIVE ELEMENTS

- poor presuppositional skills
- poor inferencing skills
- pronominal references
- lack of world knowledge regarding the following:
  - speaker
  - linguistic and physical context
  - social occasion
  - purpose of verbal interaction
  - affective variables

VISUAL AND AUDITORY ELEMENTS

- spelling cues
- punctuation cues
- faulty sending or receiving of a message

INTENTIONAL OR UNINTENTIONAL AMBIGUITY

The comment "Time flies like an arrow, fruit flies like a banana" intentionally uses the ambiguity of two words for a humorous effect. *Flies* in the first line means moving rapidly; in the second, it refers to insects. The word *like* is used in the first line to mean similar to; in the second, it means to enjoy. The use of the same words with different meanings creates the humor. The intentional use of ambiguity is the basis of many riddles, puns, jokes, comic strips, and cartoons. It also is used for capturing attention in advertisements, road signs, and so forth. Quite often, however, ambiguous comments are unintentional, such as in this headline in a golf magazine: "Grandmother of Eight Makes Hole in One." Did she accomplish a golfer's dream, or did she make a hole in one of her grandchildren? Unintentionally ambiguous utterances also can be humorous!

CONTEXTS OF AMBIGUITY

Ambiguous comments are found so frequently in our everyday lives that often we are unaware of their presence. Although we realize that our casual conversations contain many words and expressions that can be interpreted in more than one way, the pervasiveness of ambiguity in the many aspects of our lives is striking.

Check the headlines of the daily newspaper. So many of them can be confusing (or amusing) with the possibilities of dual interpretations. Consider this one: "Police Help Dog Bite Victim." Does this mean that the police came to the aid of a victim who was bitten by a dog or that the police helped the dog bite a victim? Next, turn to the sports page. The headlines read, *"NHL Trades for Muscle"* and "Yankees Are *Well Armed."* The game scores are cited: "Ducks *Whip* Blues," "Syracuse *Cuts down* Georgia." An advertisement in the newspaper asks us to come to a well-known department store because "We have a *gift* for giving." The classified advertisements provide numerous (often humorous) examples of linguistic ambiguity: "For sale: Four-poster bed. 101 years old. Perfect for *antique lover."* Or, "Dog for sale: *Eats anything—is fond of children."* Now turn to the comic strips. Hagar the Horrible is seen chasing after a swiftly running deer. "Aw, forget it," says Hagar, "I'm tired of *fast food* anyway."

Now take a ride to the supermarket and go past the flower shop, *"Petal Pushers."* The sign on a passing truck says "Acme Air Conditioners—We help you *keep your cool."* A car nearby has a bumper sticker that states, "Don't be a *bumper sticker!"* At the supermarket, there's a sign over a display of batteries that asks, "Wanna *start something?"* In the freezer are *lean meals* (sure, which way?). A pregnant shopper in the aisle is wearing a tee shirt with a downward pointing arrow under the words *"Muffin in the Oven."* On the way home, there's a sign in the window of a drug store that says, "We *dispense* with accuracy." The billboard at the side of the road states, "If you love your kid, *belt him!"*

Next, look in on Molly at school. Her teacher is discussing class behavior. "If you don't do what is expected of you, you will have to *face the music."* "Remember, you're not here to *take up space*." On the way to English literature class, Molly's friend remarks, "Ms. Johnson should *get a life."* A paragraph from Molly's textbook reads: "By three o'clock the town was *overrun* with reporters. The Norton gang had *shot its way* across five states. For a small town department to *nail* them was impossible. Kelly was already in danger of *getting fired* for *stepping on too many toes."*

At home, Molly turns on the television. "I'm leaving. I guess I never had a chance to *sow my wild oats,"* declares the character in the program she is viewing. The commercial for a shoe company shows a water pump and a banana peel on a floor. The speaker proclaims, "We have them all—*pumps, slip-ons,* you name it." An antismoking public service announcement tells the audience that tomorrow is *"kick butts"* day.

The contexts in which ambiguous language is found in just the brief preceding scenario include the following: newspapers (headlines, sports reports, advertisements, classified advertisements, comic strips), signs on vehicles and shops, bumper stickers, display signs in stores, product names, tee shirts, billboards, classroom discussions, conversations with friends, textbooks, and television dialogue and commercials. Some of these ambiguities are confusing for many (for example, "NHL Trades for Muscle" is obscure to those who do not have knowledge of sports and sporting events), others are confusing only to individuals who have difficulty understanding ambiguous language in general (such as *face the music* and *take up space*).

PROBLEMS CAUSED BY POOR UNDERSTANDING

Numerous experts have discussed the negative effect that poor understanding of ambiguous language can have on communication interactions (Boyce and Larson, 1983; Creaghead and Tattershall, 1991; Donahue and Bryan, 1984; Larson and McKinley, 1987, 1995; Nelson, 1993; Nippold, 1988; Spector, 1990, 1992; Wiig and Semel, 1984). To have normal, appropriate social interactions and academic achievement, and to be truly literate, understanding ambiguous language is imperative. The degree to which ambiguous utterances pervade our everyday lives emphasizes the need to be able to interpret such items.

ACADEMIC DIFFICULTIES

Lazar, Warr-Leeper, Beel-Nicholson, and Johnson (1989) reported that one-third of "teacher talk" is ambiguous. Given that ambiguous language is used so extensively by teachers in classroom lectures and discussions, understanding ambiguities is of considerable importance for school achievement. Students often do not respond correctly to a teacher's directions because they are too long or complex or are given too rapidly (Wiig and Semel, 1984). If, in addition, nonliteral language is used, the problem may be compounded, making directions even more difficult to follow. Certainly the ambiguities found in textbooks and other reading material will have a negative impact on comprehension if they are not understood (Nippold, 1988; Wiig and Secord, 1989).

PERSONAL AND SOCIAL DIFFICULTIES

Youths are expected to understand and use the current slang expressions, idioms, jokes, and other types of ambiguous utterances used by their peers by the time they reach adolescence. Appropriate verbal interaction with peers is important for group acceptance (Donahue and Bryan, 1984). Prutting and Kirchner (1987) and Gallagher (1991) stress the importance of considering the extent to which disruptions in conversational language are socially penalizing. The ability to use and understand slang, idioms, jokes, and puns (which so often are based on ambiguity) is necessary if unimpeded conversational interactions are to occur. Failure to use or understand these facets of language could prove to be embarrassing and could have an adverse effect on relationships with others, particularly with one's peers (Boyce and Larson, 1983; Larson and McKinley, 1987, 1995; Wiig, 1984). The desire to "fit in" with our peers is strong, especially for children and adolescents. A sense of isolation may develop for individuals who do not feel able to use or even understand the same nonliteral language used by their peers.

Inappropriate responses to polite or indirect requests could prove to be awkward or embarrassing. For example, the comment "That long walk to your house really made me thirsty" may be taken as an observation rather than a request for a beverage. The ambiguous nature of polite evasions also is a source of potential misunderstanding and embarrassment. If, for example, someone asks, "How do you like my haircut?," and the response, "It certainly is short," is not accepted, the individual may push the responder to say something that may be better left unsaid.

Dealing with sarcastic or ironic utterances also can be problematic because they involve dual meanings. Unfortunately, sarcasm is used not only by siblings and peers in their conversational interactions, but by adults to children as well. These utterances can be hurtful, especially when the recipient of the comment does not know when the speaker is joking or teasing. An individual may feel powerless to cope with social interactions that incorporate such comments (Blue, 1981). Irony, unlike sarcasm, is not necessarily negative in its effect (Milosky and Ford, 1993). For example, a proud mother praises her daughter who spent many hours studying for her math exam by using this ironic comment: "I see you did very well on your math test. Isn't it amazing how lucky you are!" Her daughter would have to recognize the irony in the comment to know that she was being complimented on the results of her efforts. At times, irony is used just to comment on the annoyances encountered in our everyday lives. The statement "No good deed goes unpunished" is ironic because we expect good deeds to be rewarded.

Complete understanding of a polite or indirect request, a polite evasion, or a sarcastic or ironic comment can occur only if the true implication of such a comment is grasped in the context in which it is made (Ackerman, 1982).

JOB-RELATED DIFFICULTIES

Going to a job interview is generally stressful. Imagine how much more stressful it is when there is concern about grasping all the figurative comments that may be made during the interview, or on the job should the results of the interview be successful. The appropriate use and understanding of nonliteral language also is needed to relate to coworkers on an equal footing. When facility with ambiguous language is lacking, verbal interactions may be stifled.

At times it is necessary to follow instructions given by a boss or other individual who has the power to promote or fire us. It is stressful, indeed, if these instructions are not understood because they are full of ambiguities. For example, a supervisor might say, "Joe, *get the lead out.* You can't *take a break* until all the reports are *put to bed*. You should *know the drill* by now," rather than, "Joe, w faster. You can't rest until all the reports are finished. You should know ι procedures by now."

In summary, an inability to understand linguistic ambiguity may lead to the following problems:

- feelings of inadequacy in understanding what everyone else seems to understand;
- embarrassment;
- impaired academic performance;
- impaired literacy;
- stifled social interactions, which may lead to a sense of isolation;
- lack of confidence about participating in verbal interactions in school, in sports, at home, or on the job;
- feeling powerless in coping with school, social, or job-related situations; and/or
- loss of the pleasure found in the many forms of humor and wordplay based on linguistic ambiguity.

POPULATIONS WHO CAN BENEFIT FROM SAYING ONE THING, MEANING ANOTHER

Individuals from a variety of populations are likely to benefit from efforts to improve their understanding and use of ambiguous language. They are described in the next five sections.

NORMALLY ACHIEVING INDIVIDUALS

Normally achieving individuals may want to improve their ability to understand utterances based on ambiguity if they find themselves frequently misunderstanding such language. This may occur as one moves to a different part of the country or changes schools, jobs, or peer groups.

It is probable that the development of skills needed to understand and appreciate the subtleties of ambiguous language continues into adulthood (Gibbs, 1987; Nippold and Martin, 1989; Prinz, 1983; Spector, 1990). These skills may still be developing in individuals who are experiencing difficulty with ambiguous language.

INDIVIDUALS WITH LANGUAGE-LEARNING DISORDERS

Individuals who have language-learning disorders (LLD) generally have poor metalinguistic skills. As a result, they frequently have difficulties dealing with ambiguous material. Difficulty with nonliteral language could adversely affect relations with siblings, peers, parents, employers, and coworkers, and it also could impact literacy and other academic pursuits (Donahue and Bryan, 1984; Larson and McKinley, 1995; Nippold, 1988; Spector, 1990; Wiig, 1984).

Given that figurative expressions and other ambiguities are so prevalent in the English language, it is apparent that simple exposure is not adequate for grasping their meaning. To ensure comprehension, many individuals with language-learning disorders need to be shown how to abstract meaning from context through repeated exposure accompanied by mediation (Nelson, 1993; Nippold, 1991).

INDIVIDUALS WITH HEARING IMPAIRMENT

Individuals with hearing impairment lack the exposure to the numerous multiple meaning words and phrases that individuals with normal hearing experience daily (Nelson, 1993). They may not hear minimal sound differences that can be crucial to understanding potentially ambiguous utterances. Important stress and intonation cues for an ambiguous word, phrase, or sentence may not be heard. Presenting these utterances to individuals with hearing impairment in an appropriate manner and with sufficiently frequent exposure has been shown to improve their thinking proficiency when dealing with problem solving and abstract language (Haywood, Towery-Woolsey, Arbitman-Smith, and Aldridge, 1988; Iran-Nejad, Ortony, and Rittenhouse, 1981; Smith, Schloss, and Israelite, 1986).

INDIVIDUALS WITH BRAIN INJURY

Individuals with brain injury have difficulty using contextual cues to help interpret language, understanding abstract language, grasping implied meaning, processing ambiguity, shifting from one meaning to another, and following rapidly spoken language (Myers, 1986). Damage to either hemisphere of the brain will affect an individual's ability to understand abstract or ambiguous language, which depends on holistic cognitive processing (McGhee, 1983). After basic communication skills are recovered, many individuals with traumatic brain injury appear to return to pretraumatic levels of functioning. However, close inspection may reveal subtle deficits in abstract, higher level cognitive skills (Haarbauer-Krupa, Henry, Szekeres, and Ylvisaker, 1985). Often there is reduced ability to understand abstractness in others' language (such as ambiguity, satire, and drawing inferences). These individuals have to be taught how to figure out the meaning of idioms and other ambiguous words and phrases (Blosser and DePompei, 1989).

INDIVIDUALS FROM CULTURALLY AND LINGUISTICALLY DIVERSE GROUPS

People from culturally and linguistically diverse groups, including individuals learning English as a second language (ESL), tend to master the morphological, phonological, and syntactic elements of language long before they understand ambiguous utterances. The interpretation of verbally or visually presented material is influenced by the individual's country of origin, its language, and its culture.

Other factors, such as gestures, eye contact, facial expressions, or body proximity of speaker and listener in a conversational interaction, often differ from one country to another and may be interpreted differently (Cheng, 1996; Owens, 1992).

Individuals from any of the populations just described often will give literal, related, tangential, or totally unrelated interpretations to the ambiguous language they read and hear. The presence of ambiguous language frequently creates unrecognized gaps in understanding. With the help of a facilitator, individuals from all of these populations can improve their understanding of ambiguous language using *Saying One Thing, Meaning Another* because it:

1. provides frequent, structured exposure to the various ambiguities;
2. presents material in a contextually supportive manner; and
3. uses a cognitive strategies approach that best facilitates learning.

A more extensive discussion of factors that affect understanding of ambiguous language for these populations is provided in Appendix A.

THE INFLUENCE OF COGNITIVE LEARNING THEORIES

Cognitive learning theories have influenced the teaching approach—a cognitive strategies approach—implemented in this resource. Cognitive learning theories, which provide a basis for making decisions about goals and procedures and for effecting a positive change in language behaviors, offer the following for facilitators:

- ideas about what an individual ought to be able to learn;
- ideas about the order in which language abilities are acquired; and
- indications of the types of activities that best facilitate learning.

Principles of both *constructivist-cognitive* (Case, 1985; Fischer and Pipp, 1984; Karmiloff-Smith, 1979; Piaget, 1985; Pinker, 1991) and *social-cognitive* (Reid, 1988; van Kleeck and Richardson, 1986; Vygotsky, 1962) learning theories provide the foundation for the cognitive strategies approach used in *Saying One Thing, Meaning Another*. For a discussion of these learning theories and their influence on developing a cognitive strategies approach, as well as citations for the research related to these theories, see Appendix B.

COGNITIVE STRATEGIES APPROACH

The following guiding principles of a cognitive strategies approach will enable professionals to get the most beneficial results from their efforts to facilitate language learning:

- consider the individual's current level of development or functioning;
- adjust assistance to fit the needs of the individual, taking interests and past experiences into account;
- assist the individual in learning the process of identifying the steps in an activity;
- mediate an activity's level of difficulty so that an individual can realize greater levels of competency without being overwhelmed;
- assist the individual in expanding (or regaining) world knowledge;
- assist the individual in developing pragmatic skills, such as knowing "when to say what";
- assist the individual in developing problem-solving procedures;
- promote the individual's ability to make inferences;
- present materials in varying formats that are consistent with the individual's interests;
- assist the individual in the development (or regaining) of reasoning skills;
- whenever possible, provide naturalistic contexts; and
- assist in the development of repair strategies when there is a miscommunication of meaning.

The issue of assisting individuals who have lost language skills through brain injury or assisting individuals who are learning English as a second language has not specifically been addressed in this context. However, it seems reasonable that following the principles of constructivist-cognitive and social-cognitive learning theories will have a positive effect on their learning as well.

TEACHING TASK-SPECIFIC COGNITIVE STRATEGIES

A cognitive strategies training approach involves teaching individuals to adopt conscious strategies of problem solving—that is, to direct their own learning. The intervention materials developed for *Saying One Thing, Meaning Another* are based on a cognitive strategies approach suggested by Seidenberg (1988). The goals in this approach are to

- improve the individual's awareness of the task demands;
- help the individual find the relevant strategy;
- describe the strategy to the individual; and
- help the individual apply the strategy in controlled practice materials.

Numerous experts have discussed task-specific cognitive strategies training. Their findings are as follows:

1. It is possible to successfully teach task-specific cognitive strategies (de Bettencourt, 1987; Gelzheiser, 1984; Pflaum and Pascarella, 1980; Schumaker, Deshler, Alley, Warner, and Denton, 1984; Sternberg, Okagaki, and Jackson, 1990; Wong and Jones, 1982).

2. Once individuals acquire strategies, they can be taught to generalize what they have learned to other, similar situations (Larson and McKinley, 1987, 1995; McKinley and Larson, 1985; Nippold, 1991).

3. Strategies training is especially important for individuals with language learning problems because they appear to have difficulty acquiring such strategies on their own (Buttrill, Niizawa, Biemer, Takakashi, and Hearn, 1989; Pehrsson and Denner, 1988; Schumaker, Deshler, Alley, and Warner, 1983).

4. The logical organization of material (structure) influences learning even when the learner is not aware of the effects. However, learning is maximized when the learner is aware of important features of the material being considered (Seidenberg, 1988).

"META" SKILLS AND DEVELOPING COMMUNICATIVE COMPETENCE

A group of "meta" skills (affecting the ability to "know that you know") are involved in developing communicative competence. They are *metacognition*, *metapragmatics*, and *metalinguistics*. For a communicative interaction (ambiguous or otherwise) to be meaningful, skills from all three "meta" categories are required.

METACOGNITIVE SKILLS

Metacognition is knowledge about one's own cognitive processes, such as knowing about attending, organizing, remembering, and problem solving. Metacognition also involves knowing that there are strategies for making these processes more efficient. Using this knowledge in learning tasks is the dynamic dimension of metacognition (Ylvisaker and Szekeres, 1989). For example, "thinking aloud" when performing a task makes use of an individual's awareness of a problem-solving strategy: "The lid on the peanut butter jar is on too tight. I can't get it off. I can't ask Mom, she's out shopping. Maybe if I bang on the lid it will loosen up. That didn't work. If I use this towel, maybe I can get a better grip on the jar and the lid." This type of verbal problem solving encourages the individual to explore all possible options, to consider similar situations related to opening a jar, and to remember what worked. Once the problem-solving options are verbalized, the individual can then consider other options that may have been overlooked. Further efforts in solving this problem might include developing an alternate solution (such as asking a neighborhood friend's mom or dad to help open the jar, or eating something else). An awareness of problem-solving strategies is needed for interpreting ambiguous language. The use of a reflective problem-solving style is related to competence with ambiguous material (Nippold, 1988).

METAPRAGMATIC SKILLS

Metapragmatics involves an individual's conscious awareness of the cultural rules for using language efficiently in various social contexts (van Kleeck, 1987). Awareness of pragmatic variables, such as requesting information, responding appropriately to a question or request, or revising an ambiguous message, is an integral part of meaningful communication with others. Consider, for example, how confused we would be if a friend said, "Bring a *bibble* when you come to my house tomorrow." Only by requesting clarifying information ("What is a bibble?") could we determine the meaning of our friend's comment.

METALINGUISTIC SKILLS

The abilities to reflect on language as an entity and to analyze language into its linguistic components are aspects of *metalinguistic awareness* (van Kleeck, 1984). Lloyd (1994) pointed out that the difficulty many individuals have in detecting ambiguity in messages may be caused by undeveloped metalinguistic skills. Our ability to monitor our own comprehension comes from growth in metalinguistic awareness. It includes the ability to appraise incoming information effectively as well as the ability to monitor responses of a conversational partner. It also includes the ability to give appropriate feedback to the speaker so that clarifications can be made when there is a misunderstanding.

Metalinguistic skills development is a long, ongoing process that takes several years. In fact, the gradual development of these skills continues into adulthood (Gibbs, 1987; Nippold and Martin, 1989; Prinz, 1983).

Many children and adolescents with language disorders have not adequately developed their metalinguistic skills. Individuals who have sustained brain injury frequently experience impairment of these skills.

SKILLS NEEDED TO UNDERSTAND AND USE AMBIGUOUS LANGUAGE

Metacognitive abilities for activities such as attending, organizing, remembering, and problem solving affect the development of metalinguistic skills. Metapragmatic abilities for activities such as requesting information or revising an utterance also affect the development of metacognitive and metalinguistic skills. No clear-cut lines of distinction can be drawn among these domains of awareness. Each will have some impact on the others. Skills needed for the understanding and use of ambiguous language appear in bold type in the narrative that follows.

To **detect the presence** of an ambiguous word, phrase, or idiomatic exp
one must have the ability to **recognize it from stored memory.** Metalingui
also is required for **evoking new and different meanings in words and phrases, and for interpreting them literally and figuratively** (Nippold and Fey, 1983; Lee and Kamhi, 1985). For example, it is necessary to understand the multiple meanings of a word in this joke: "There was a man here to see you." "Did he have a *bill?*" "No, just a regular nose." Or, for the following humorous comment, "The trouble with being inhibited is that you're all *tied up in nots,*" it would be necessary not only to **recognize** the idiom, but also to **analyze** and **integrate** the role played by the alternate spelling (homophone) of the word *nots* (knots).

Defining words with more than one meaning may require the ability to make more definitive distinctions. The individual words learned as children as having one particular meaning can take on new, and often subtle, meanings as lexical knowledge is expanded. For example, the word *cloud* is commonly learned by children to mean a mass of moisture in the sky ("Look at that big *cloud*. It looks like we might have some rain"). As children mature, they learn that *cloud* can mean to obscure ("Don't *cloud* the issue") or to cast gloom over ("His remark cast a *cloud* over her day"). Children often know more about words than they can actually explain (Nippold, 1988). Defining words is a skill that can be developed with modeled examples and numerous experiences in providing definitions. The more experience the individual has in defining words, the easier it becomes to produce clearer, more accurate definitions (Watson, 1985). However, there are too many multiple meaning words to ever teach them all directly. The individual must be able to

- recognize instances of multiple word meaning;
- realize that word meanings vary as a function of context; and
- understand that some words have specialized meanings for particular subjects.

To **analyze syntactic information**, the individual must be able to reflect on, and make sense of, the form of an utterance as it relates to the content. While gathering a spontaneous language sample for a language development course, Lauren, an undergraduate student, had the following conversation with a three-year-old boy:

Lauren: Mommy tells me that you just came from a birthday party.

Timmy: Uh-huh. It was Jamie's birthday.

Lauren: Oh. How old is he now?

Timmy: *He is a she!*

The skills required for showing comprehension of the ambiguity of idioms are especially challenging. As Nippold and Rudzinski (1993) have pointed out, it is not easy "to reflect upon the meaning of a lexical unit and to state explicitly what is known implicitly" (p. 735). An individual would have to be able to **explain multiple meanings** for a group of words that mean something other than the sum of the meanings of the individual words, **integrate contextual information** from the material in which the idiom is embedded, and **put into words what is implicitly known.** For example, the idiom *hold up* is the ambiguity in the following verbal exchange: "How do you know that robbers are very strong?" "They *hold up* banks." While the word *strong* gives contextual support for the literal interpretation of actually lifting the bank building in the air, it is the word *robbers*, a word closely associated with *hold up,* that lends contextual support for the appropriate figurative interpretation. Yet another metalinguistic skill would be to **recognize** the idiom **as familiar from its use in other contexts** such as television shows and movies.

Contrary to the view that idioms are learned as giant lexical units (Ackerman, 1982; Hoffman and Honeck, 1980), Gibbs (1987) and Nippold and Rudzinski (1993) have found that some idioms (such as *skating on thin ice*) are relatively transparent and can be figured out from the words that comprise the idiom. The individual words in *skating on thin ice* lead us to **infer** the figurative **meaning** of being in danger.

Often we are unaware of the amount of inferencing we are required to use in our everyday conversations. When we are asked, "Do you have the time?" we infer that the true meaning of the request is "If you know the time, tell me." If we are asked, "Do you know the way to San Jose?" we could say yes or no, but we infer that the true intent of the questioner is to obtain directions. Indirect requests put even more of a strain on our inferencing skills. "My, but it's warm in here" may be a statement of fact, but is often an indirect way of saying "Someone please open the window" or "Someone please turn on the air conditioner." We can draw the appropriate inference of such messages by **using the context** in which the message is embedded, by **using vocal (paralinguistic) cues** such as stress and intonation, and by **using other nonverbal cues** such as the facial expression or body language of the speaker or gestures that accompany the utterance.

If an utterance is unclear, **paraphrasing** often will remove the ambiguity. For example, the following utterance, "My brother Jim has grown another foot," could be interpreted to mean that Jim will now need three socks. By paraphrasing in the following manner, the utterance becomes unambiguous: "My brother Jim has grown a foot taller." The individual must be able to recognize that a comment restated in a paraphrased form conveys the same information and may clarify meaning as well.

If changes in stress or intonation patterns in a word, phrase, or sentence cause ambiguity, it is necessary to **segment and redefine a phonological string** without the support of underlying meaning (Spector, 1990). "Knock-knock" jokes, for example, frequently are based on this type of linguistic manipulation: "Knock-knock." "Who's there?" "Dewey." "Dewey who?" "Dewey have to tell knock-knock jokes?" The word *Dewey* has to be resegmented into *do we* to discern the appropriate interpretation.

When confusion occurs in a conversational interaction, it is important that we have the skill to **revise** the utterance to **accommodate the listener's needs.** When conversing with an individual with impaired hearing, for example, we may have to use a louder voice or look directly at the individual as we speak. When talking with children, we would have to consider whether the vocabulary and syntax are age appropriate or whether the sentences are too lengthy. Awareness of what the listener needs to fully understand a message, whether ambiguous or not, is based on the ability to **shift perspective.** Being able to take the speaker's perspective is a social-cognitive skill of particular importance in understanding the indirect comments, polite evasions, and ironic and sarcastic comments that occur frequently in everyday conversations.

Unless each individual involved in a conversation is able to **monitor the message** and **repair any breakdown** that may occur, there will be a lack of understanding on the part of the listener. Normally, when a communication breakdown occurs, the conversational partners request clarification or restatement of the utterance (using repetition, rephrasing, a louder voice, and so forth). In the case of a speaker wrongly assuming (presupposing) that the listener has background knowledge needed to understand an utterance, the speaker must **recognize the listener's confusion** by observing and interpreting body language and facial expressions and provide the necessary information relating to the prior situation or prior utterances made. The ability to **provide appropriate revision** so the listener understands the message is another important metalinguistic skill. The numerous skills involved in understanding and using ambiguous language are summarized in Table 2 on page 18.

WORLD KNOWLEDGE AND UNDERSTANDING AMBIGUITY

Language is filled with potential ambiguities—phonological, syntactic, semantic, and pragmatic. Words can have numerous meanings or senses, and when combined with the senses of other words, can generate many potential meanings for any one sentence (Milosky, 1990). For example, "Joe entered the institution" could be interpreted in numerous ways depending upon the relevant information (world knowledge) available. There are many ways to define *enter* and *institution*. Webster's dictionary offers the following definitions:

enter: come in(to), approach, board, break in, penetrate, enroll, register, matriculate, begin, launch, join, pledge oneself, record

SKILLS NEEDED TO UNDERSTAND AND USE AMBIGUOUS LANGUAGE

- detect the presence of ambiguous material
- recognize ambiguous material from stored memory
- evoke new and different meanings in words, phrases, and sentences
- interpret ambiguous materials literally and figuratively
- analyze and integrate contextual information
- define words
- analyze and integrate syntactic information
- explain multiple meanings
- integrate contextual information
- put into words what is known implicitly
- generalize meaning from use in other contexts
- infer meaning
- perceive and use paralinguistic cues (i.e., vocal intensity, stress, intonation)
- perceive and use nonverbal cues (i.e., facial expressions, body language, gestures)
- paraphrase to clarify meaning
- segment and redefine a phonological string
- revise an utterance to fulfill the listener's needs
- perceive shifts in perspective
- monitor one's own utterances
- recognize a listener's inability to understand an utterance
- provide appropriate repairs of communication breakdown

institution: establishment, custom, practice, association, society, medical center, sanitarium, museum, academy, business, corporation, bank

The following are all potential interpretations for "Joe entered the institution":

- Joe enrolled in a college.
- Joe broke into the bank.
- Joe went to jail.
- Joe registered the historic landmark.
- Joe joined the Rotary club.
- Joe went to the sanitarium.
- Joe penetrated the FBI.
- Joe walked into the building.

So how do we determine which of these interpretations is appropriate in any particular verbal interaction? We must see how the message we are receiving is relevant to what we already know about the context or situation. If we know Joe is a crook, then "Joe broke into the bank" or "Joe went to jail" may be the correct interpretations. If Joe's health has been steadily deteriorating, then "Joe went to the sanitarium" is a logical interpretation.

What we know is taken from our fund of world knowledge. We gain our world knowledge through experience, and we selectively activate what is deemed to be relevant (Milosky, 1990). As Milosky pointed out, what gets activated in the process of understanding is determined by an intermingling of the following factors: knowledge of the speaker, linguistic and physical context, the social occasion, the purpose of the verbal interaction, and affective variables. The facilitator's goal, therefore, should be to help the individual access and add to knowledge which is deemed relevant for understanding a spoken interaction.

The world knowledge base for speakers of English as a second language generally is formed in their country of origin. For these individuals, it is not so much a matter of developing skills as it is of expanding their base of world knowledge relevant to their adopted country and increasing appropriately structured exposure to the ambiguities in the English language.

KNOWLEDGE OF THE SPEAKER

Words alone do not give the sense of an utterance. We need to use what we know about the speaker, the speaker's state of mind, and what the speaker's goals might be before an utterance can be properly interpreted.

When two people engaging in a conversation know each other, they generally have a base of shared knowledge. This knowledge can be used when interpreting the speaker's comments, especially when the comments' real meanings have to be inferred, such as in humorous remarks, sarcastic comments, indirect requests, or evasive responses for the sake of politeness. The better listeners know the speaker, the better they perceive the speaker's intentions. For example, a young man, Ted, asks Jane out for dinner. Although Jane is not really busy, she does not want to go to dinner with Ted and offers this polite evasion: "Sorry, I've already made other plans." How well Ted knows Jane will enable him to determine whether she really is busy or whether this is a brush-off. If, on the other hand, Jane is anxious to get rid of Ted, she might respond with a more obvious refusal: "Sorry, I have to clip my toenails." In this context, the message is undoubtedly intended to be sarcastic, and Ted should get the message whether he knows Jane well or not.

CONTEXT—LINGUISTIC AND PHYSICAL

Unless a discussion is just beginning, we interpret what we hear in relation to whatever topic has already been established. When a topic is not consistent with prior comments, its meaning may be obscured. For example, without contextual cues, the following comment is completely ambiguous: "John did not see a sole." If presented in verbal form, where spelling is not a consideration, the word *sole* could also be thought of as *soul*. What did John not see: a person, a spiritual entity, a fish, or a part of a shoe? However, if the prior discussion (linguistic context) concerned John's efforts to repair a shoe, the meaning becomes clear. Or, if we knew that John works in a shoe repair shop, and not a fish market, we also would know the meaning of *sole* because our knowledge of the physical environment eliminates the ambiguity. Another example of how context supports meaning is seen when interpreting this statement: "Go find the table." It would be simple to determine its meaning if one knew that the speaker is standing next to a set of four chairs in a furniture store. The physical context provides the appropriate information. If the speaker is in an office setting, "Go find the table" may refer to a piece of furniture or a written document. Although the physical setting of the furniture store offered an excellent clue, the linguistic context of prior utterances, such as comments relating to the putting together of an annual report, is needed in the office setting.

When both speaker and listener are in the same setting, they can rely on the physical surroundings to promote understanding in their interactions. However, when interactions take place on the telephone or in two different rooms, or if the speaker and listener do not have access within a room to the same visual field, they must rely on the listener to take the speaker's perspective in order to understand the speaker.

Speakers must adjust their messages according to what they presuppose their listeners already know. They have to sense what the listener needs to know to understand and respond (Bloom and Lahey, 1978). Barrier game activities have been used to foster the development of such skills (Bunce, 1989; Dickson, 1983). For example, assume a large poster board is placed between two individuals seated at a table. Neither individual can see anything on the other side of the board. Each individual has an identical set of toy animals, and each animal is available in different sizes and colors. The first individual directs the second to "put the elephant under the bear." The second individual is not certain which bear to move over which elephant, since neither color nor size were specified. Alternatively, the first individual could have appropriately judged what was needed for compliance with the request and said, "Put the small white elephant under the big brown bear." The listener, on the other hand, could have requested clarifying information.

PREVIOUS EXPERIENCES

An individual's background will affect the way in which he or she interprets verbal information. At first glance, a comment such as "He had a ball," without benefit of additional information, would probably hold different meaning for a ballplayer (spherical object), a child who attends birthday parties (a good time), or an organizer of charity affairs (a large, formal dance). Individuals should be encouraged to go beyond the first impression caused by their own background knowledge and consider all other possibilities.

The fact that words or phrases are generally understood most easily when they are embedded in familiar contexts provides us with a valuable teaching concept.

Placing new words and phrases in familiar contexts is likely to enhance an individual's ability to learn them.

LEVEL OF INVOLVEMENT

An individual's ability to focus attention, comprehend information, and retain information is related to whether the tasks involved are seen to be relevant and of personal interest. If learning tasks are presented in situations that are meaningful, an individual will be more likely to learn and retain the material.

Helping individuals to understand ambiguous material taken from everyday life is the goal of *Saying One Thing, Meaning Another*. How well this goal is achieved is affected by each individual's emotional involvement. An individual's level of involvement with the intervention materials will affect his or her level of learning. Nelson (1988), Pellegrini and Galda (1982), and Milosky (1990) found this to be true for children. It is likely to be true for adolescents and adults as well.

Our ability to understand how linguistic elements are being manipulated to create ambiguity is advanced by world knowledge in its many forms. We must access what is already known from past experiences and explore what is not yet known. Abilities such as inferring what a speaker has in mind, knowing what the listener needs to know to understand the message, and discerning relevant contextual cues in interpreting a message are not just helpful adjuncts to learning. They are essential for attaining true comprehension.

Table 3 on the next page summarizes the points raised in this discussion about world knowledge. The table also offers suggestions for using this information.

LEARNING AMBIGUOUS MATERIAL

CONTEXTUAL SUPPORT

Are ambiguous utterances embedded in spontaneous conversations easier to understand than those embedded in contrived materials? This question has been addressed by Berlin, Blank, and Rose (1980), who contended that ambiguities embedded in a spontaneous language context may be difficult to grasp amid a complex and often rapid flow of language. The individual has little time to focus on an utterance and consider its ambiguous nature. On the other hand, Wallach and Lee (1980) pointed out that a spontaneous language context offers facial expressions, gestures, body language, and intonational and situational cues that may help convey the meaning of the utterance.

Individuals who need to improve their understanding of ambiguous language have already been exposed to the ambiguities in their "natural" environment. Their difficulty in mastering this aspect of language on their own indicates that a

Table 3

WORLD KNOWLEDGE FACTORS

WORLD KNOWLEDGE FACTS	SUGGESTIONS FOR THE FACILITATOR
1. We selectively activate information that we deem to be relevant from our fund of world knowledge.	1. Help the individual access and add to knowledge that is relevant for understanding the particular verbal interaction.
2. Our skill in understanding the ambiguity of linguistic elements is affected by how well we use our world knowledge.	2. Use all available world knowledge when examining utterances, especially those that are indirect and that require varying types of nonliteral interpretations.
3. Individuals engaged in conversation generally have a base of shared knowledge that can be used to interpret comments whose real meaning must be inferred.	3. Discuss what is known about the speaker and the speaker's goals for the particular interaction.
4. Prior utterances provide linguistic context. The setting, or knowledge of the setting, provides physical context.	4. When linguistic or physical contextual information is not available, help the individual learn to adjust the message to provide what the listener needs to know in order to understand and to respond.
5. An individual's background will affect the way in which verbal information is interpreted. Words and phrases are generally understood most easily in contexts most familiar to the individual.	5. Embed new words and phrases in familiar contexts to enhance learning.
6. The individual's ability to learn is related to the individual's level of involvement with the learning tasks.	6. Use materials that are relevant and of personal interest to the individual.
7. Ambiguity often can be resolved when the individual adjusts the message to repair breakdowns in communication.	7. Make the individual aware of repair strategies for breakdowns in communication, such as rephrasing or adding the necessary information.
8. When linguistic or physical context cues are unavailable, use whatever information can be gathered by looking at the speaker and listening to the tone of the message.	8. Help the individual use visual and auditory cues such as facial expression, gestures, body language, and tone of voice.

facilitator is needed to provide the opportunities and structure for learning (Brown, Anderson, Shillcock, and Yule, 1984). Individuals who have problems understanding abstract or ambiguous language because they have poor metalinguistic awareness are likely to achieve greater success with a facilitator (teacher) than they would by working on their own.

The use of contrived materials with appropriate, well-developed contextual support appears to be the logical solution. Basic skills needed for understanding ambiguities can be established in activities developed especially for that purpose. Larson and McKinley (1995) suggest that such materials be developed along a continuum that eventually leads to understanding in natural settings.

At first, a great deal of information (contextual cueing) is needed to lead an individual to the correct interpretation of an ambiguous utterance. For example, "Lyle is always boasting about one thing or another. He loves to give his opinion, even when he doesn't know what he is talking about. He just loves to talk. If you know a secret that you don't want anyone to know, don't tell Lyle. It's hard to stop him from *shooting off his mouth.*" The context of this story not only supports the idiom *shooting off his mouth,* it also defines it (to boast or talk too much; to tell someone's secrets). A less supportive context would be, "Oh, don't pay any attention to Lyle. He's always *shooting off his mouth.*" The context does not provide much support, and based on the comment "Don't pay any attention to Lyle," we would have to tax our inferencing skills to realize that *shooting off his mouth* means Lyle talks too much or is saying the wrong thing. Eventually, less and less contextual support is needed as an individual becomes more adept at using all available linguistic and nonlinguistic cues.

FREQUENCY OF OCCURRENCE

The more frequently an ambiguity is heard in spontaneous conversation, the more familiar it will become. However, familiarity is not in itself a sufficient condition for understanding the meaning of an ambiguity. Appropriate contextual support is essential. In conversations, we often hear ambiguities that can have a multitude of meanings. This broad exposure, or frequency of hearing the phrase, may make it easy to understand, but only if contextual support is available for the interpretation that is appropriate. Consider the word *square,* for example. *Square* could be interpreted in multiple ways:

- having equal sides and four right angles (a shape);
- raised to the second power (a mathematical operation);
- of a shape suggesting strength and solidarity (squarely built);
- having unsophisticated or conservative tastes or views ("He's a square");
- straightforward and honest ("She's always square with everyone");
- substantial, satisfying (a square meal); and

- leaving no balance, settling an account ("You have no more debt; we're square").

Without contextual information, no matter how frequently we hear the word *square*, we do not really know how it is to be interpreted.

Some ambiguous utterances are used by some groups and not by others. Therefore, one's degree of familiarity with any particular ambiguity also will depend on its usage by individuals in a particular age group, cultural group, or geographic location.

2

PREINTERVENTION AND INTERVENTION CONSIDERATIONS

TYPES OF AMBIGUITY ADDRESSED IN *SAYING ONE THING, MEANING ANOTHER*

This book provides intervention materials for four types of ambiguity. The first type includes multiple meaning words that are homographs (a word that sounds the same and is spelled the same as another word but has a different meaning), and multiple meaning words that are homophones (a word that sounds the same as another word but has a different meaning *and* a different spelling). Multiple meaning words are considered to be the easiest of the four types of ambiguity.

Sentences that can be taken in two ways are the second type of ambiguity. In these sentences, more than one set relationship can exist among the words and phrases. Also included in this category are indirect or polite requests, polite evasions, and ironic and sarcastic comments, in which the ambiguity is caused by the speaker's intentions rather than by manipulation of the linguistic elements.

Multiple meaning phrases, mainly idioms, are the third type of ambiguity. Some idioms have only one meaning (such as *fall in love*), some have two (such as *down in the dumps*), and others have many (such as *hold up*). Some idioms are transparent, and their meanings can be inferred by examining the words that comprise them. Other idioms are opaque, and each of these must be learned as a giant lexical unit.

The fourth type of ambiguity is that caused by changes in stress and/or juncture. This type of ambiguity is considered to be the most difficult to understand because it requires the coordination of several metalinguistic skills (e.g., detecting the presence of an ambiguity and then segmenting and redefining a phonological string without the support of underlying meaning).

RATIONALE FOR SELECTING AND PRESENTING INTERVENTION MATERIALS

A major goal for *Saying One Thing, Meaning Another* is to provide intervention materials in a practical, enjoyable, and readily applicable format:

- Materials selected for examining the ambiguities in this book are taken from everyday life. Whenever possible, the actual ambiguous item is used. Otherwise, the item is contrived to be as close as possible to the item as it would be in a natural situation. Some story contexts, for example, are similar to those in textbooks, but they are structured so that, at first, there is a great deal of contextual support provided to assist in interpreting the ambiguity.

- Ambiguities in this text are arranged in a hierarchical manner. The easiest type, multiple meaning words, is introduced first, followed by sentences with two meanings (including those caused by speakers' intentions, which are the most difficult of this type of ambiguity), multiple meaning phrases (for example, idioms), and finally the most difficult, ambiguities caused by changes in stress and/or juncture.

- The indirect or polite requests, polite evasions, and ironic or sarcastic comments included in this resource have been taken, whenever possible, from actual utterances this author has heard. Some of the utterances are "reasonable facsimiles."

- For the first few activities in the chapters addressing multiple meaning words (Chapter 3) and multiple meaning phrases (Chapter 5), the ambiguous word or phrase is highlighted. Thereafter, the individual must locate the ambiguity. The nature of the items addressing changes in stress and/or juncture and dual-meaning sentences makes them unsuitable candidates for highlighting. Highlighting stress and/or juncture items would eliminate one of the major goals of Chapter 6, that of detecting the phonological string that must be segmented and redefined to find the ambiguity. Highlighting items in the dual-sentences chapter (Chapter 4) would be pointless, as the entire item would be highlighted.

- Given that much of the humor, advertisements, bumper stickers, tee shirts, and so forth to which we are exposed are based on ambiguity, *Saying One Thing, Meaning Another* makes extensive use of these types of items. These materials provide individuals seeking to improve their competence in understanding ambiguity with opportunities for

    1. developing problem-solving skills;
    2. enhancing their divergent thinking skills;
    3. benefitting from ongoing verbal mediation and supportive discussion;
    4. expanding their world knowledge;
    5. improving their visual awareness;
    6. increasing their vocabulary; and
    7. enjoying intervention sessions more.

In addition, the use of humor has two particular benefits worth noting: The first is that an individual's competence with ambiguous sentences is enhanced by picture cues (Nippold, 1988) like those in cartoons and comic strips. The second is that humor generally creates a relaxed atmosphere that is likely to facilitate learning.

ABOUT CONTEXT CLUES

Some of the activities in *Saying One Thing, Meaning Another* are specifically designed to provide context clues that support the intended meaning of a word, phrase, or sentence. However, the context clues available for other activities (such as those in jokes, riddles, signs, advertisements, cartoons, comic strips, and so forth) cannot be manipulated. They are inherent to the items. Some provide clues that support literal interpretations, some provide clues that support figurative interpretations, and some provide clues that support two different interpretations. Context clues are unique to each item.

The following are examples of the types of context clues found in this resource:

- Two cannibal chiefs were talking during dinner: "Your wife makes a wonderful pot roast." "Yes," replied the second chief. "And I'm certainly going to miss her."

The word *cannibal* provides a clue for the literal interpretation. (The second chief's wife was the pot roast.)

- The clue in this cartoon supports the literal interpretation of *eating like a bird*. The woman has her head and body bent down and she is pecking at her food the way a bird would.

- Rachel: "I'm so annoyed with Joe. I asked him to give me a hand after I slipped on the ice."

  Sarah: "Why are you annoyed?"

  Rachel: "He stood there and applauded."

  The clue in this joke, *applauded,* supports a figurative meaning of the phrase *give me a hand*. The alternate meaning is *help me*, but that also is figurative.

- The clues in this cartoon support a figurative interpretation of the phrase *break a leg* (meaning *good luck* in show business). The little girl is wearing a ballet costume, and the sign says "Dance recital."

- The clues in the cartoon above support both interpretations of the question, "Coffee?" Hagar's wife stands near him, ready to pour coffee from the pot ("Do you want coffee?"), and Hagar looks into the pot to see what is in it ("Is this coffee?").

- The clues in this cartoon, a fork used as an eating utensil and a road that divides into two branches, support both interpretations of *a fork in the road*.

USING EXPLANATION TASKS TO ANALYZE AMBIGUOUS LANGUAGE

Activities in *Saying One Thing, Meaning Another* require individuals to explain ambiguities even though researchers have found that explanation tasks, especially for showing comprehension of figurative language such as idioms, metaphors, and proverbs, are more difficult than multiple- or forced-choice formats (Gibbs, 1987; Nippold, 1985; Nippold, Martin, and Erskine, 1988; Nippold and Rudzinski, 1993; Nippold, Uhden, and Schwarz, 1997; Prinz, 1983; Winner, Engel, and Gardner, 1980). The consensus is that explanation tasks may underestimate understanding in assessment procedures, and the use of multiple- or forced-choice formats allows the individual to show comprehension in a passive manner. However, there are several reasons for using explanation tasks in intervention activities such as those found in this resource:

1. To provide explanations, an individual must develop the metalinguistic skills needed for active rather than passive understanding and for communicating meaning in a clear manner. According to Vygotsky's (1962) theory, if these skills are perceived as being weak, it is possible to facilitate their development.

2. Often explanations are required in "real life" situations. Generally, multiple choices are not offered. Gaining experience with explanation tasks involving ambiguities can be a useful method of improving one's ability to provide explanations in other language areas.

3. The nature of some items do not lend themselves to multiple-choice formats. Stress and intonation items, for example, are based on one's ability to select a phonological string and resegment it to form a new meaning. A multiple-choice format would compromise the selection procedure.

4. Explanations frequently are needed in academic subjects. Although explanations may underestimate passive understanding, they allow the facilitator to gain insight into qualitative changes as the individual continues to work on a specific language task. Facilitators would then have the opportunity to examine the explanation and determine what is needed to provide true understanding.

ASSESSING UNDERSTANDING OF AMBIGUITIES

INFORMAL ASSESSMENT

An individual's understanding of each type of ambiguity can be informally measured before and after he or she uses the intervention materials in *Saying One Thing, Meaning Another*. Select three items from each of the ambiguity chapters (Chapters 3 through 6) before intervention and three different items from each of these chapters after intervention. Selection of the items should be random.

STANDARDIZED ASSESSMENT

Facilitators who prefer standardized tests to assess comprehension and use of ambiguities will find some forms of ambiguous language in these four tests:

- *Test of Language Competence–Expanded Edition* (for ages 9:0 to 18:11) by Wiig and Secord (1989) contains subtests that assess the understanding of linguistic ambiguity and figurative language.

- *Test of Word Knowledge* (for ages 5:0 to 18:0) by Wiig and Secord (1992) contains subtests that assess comprehension and explanation of multiple meaning words and multiple meanings of phrases (i.e., idioms).

- *The Fullerton Language Test for Adolescents* (Second Edition) (for ages 11 to 18) by Thorum (1986) contains a subtest that assesses explanation of idioms.

- *The Word Test–Revised* (for ages 7 to 11) by Huisingh, Barrett, Zachman, Blagden, and Orman (1990) assesses explanation of multiple meaning words.

DEVELOPING INDIVIDUALIZED EDUCATIONAL PROGRAMS (IEPS)

Facilitators who work in school settings may need to develop IEPs. Appendix C lists suggested goals and objectives that relate to each type of ambiguity specifically and to ambiguity in general (semantic and pragmatic language skills).

PRESENTING THE INTERVENTION ACTIVITIES

Chapters 3–6 in *Saying One Thing, Meaning Another* each present a set of activities addressing one of the four types of ambiguity. Chapter 7 presents a set of activities for clarifying ambiguous utterances. All of these activities are appropriate for one-to-one or group interactions. While one-to-one interactions may be more highly focused on the needs of the individual, working with groups offers increased opportunities for "brainstorming" sessions.

The first page of each activity (or section of activities) includes the directions and usually one or more examples. Examples are preceded by a bullet point. Example tasks are presented for teaching and discussion before individual or group work on specific types of ambiguity. The answers to the examples are provided in the answer key at the end of each chapter.

Some activities continue for several lessons, and these pages are headed with Roman numerals (for example, Dual-Meaning Sentences I, II, and III). The Roman numerals do not imply a hierarchy of difficulty. Rather, they serve as a means to controlling the length of any one set of reproducible activity pages. Usually the directions corresponding to any pages with Roman numeral headings precede the first task.

When presenting the activities, use the following guidelines:

1. Based on assessment results, choose the appropriate chapter(s) for intervention activities.

2. Duplicate the items for each of the activities chosen. Distribute to each individual a copy of the items for the particular activity that is to be attempted. When working with groups, an alternative is to make transparencies and use an overhead projector.

3. Read the directions and work together to complete the example item(s). When warranted, facilitate a discussion about the ambiguity.

4. Decide whether to read and complete the items together or to have the individuals read and complete them alone. This decision should be based on what would be most beneficial for each individual. Consider reading skills, visual acuity, and so forth. When possible, it is best for individuals to see each item as well as hear it read aloud.

5. Decide whether responses to stimulus items will be written or oral. Again, this decision should be based on what is best for each individual. The mode of presenting the items (on individual pages or on an overhead projector) also will affect this decision.

6. Discuss the responses to each item. If desired, compare each individual's responses with those in the answer key.

7. Remember the chapters are arranged in a hierarchical manner (i.e., Chapter 3 is easier than Chapter 4, Chapter 4 is easier than Chapter 5, etc.). However, within any chapter there may be items which are quite subtle (such as ironic and sarcastic comments) and not appropriate for every individual. The individual's age and current level of language functioning should be considered when determining the suitability of particular stimulus items.

8. Encourage individuals to try several of each type of item before determining that any type is inappropriate.

9. Be aware that several activities in Chapter 5 (Multiple Meaning Phrases) will require the use of an idiom or proverb dictionary.

10. Utilize the glossary at the end of this book. It serves as a resource for facilitators when defining terms related to ambiguous language.

GENERAL SUGGESTIONS FOR FACILITATORS

In addition to the steps described, these general suggestions may be helpful when presenting the activities.

- *Verbal mediation.* In the early stages of intervention, offer a great deal of ongoing verbal mediation. Use the examples at the beginning of each activity to fully discuss possible responses to each question so that a correct pattern of response is set for the activity items. Continue to offer verbal mediation as long as necessary.

- *Thinking aloud.* Have individuals "think aloud" when attempting to figure out potentially problematic ambiguous material. In this way, (a) alternate meanings can be considered, (b) points of confusion can be identified, (c) context clues can be pointed out and discussed, (d) analogies can be drawn to what is already known, and (e) repair strategies can be used when there is a failure to comprehend.

- *Paraphrasing.* Paraphrasing is an excellent strategy for revealing the alternate meaning of an ambiguous word or sentence. Ask individuals to read the ambiguous item, such as a joke, a newspaper headline, a road sign, an advertisement, or a cartoon, and paraphrase what is actually being said. For example, "When John was away at school, he grew another foot." In its paraphrased form, the intended meaning of the word *foot* becomes clear: "When John was away at school, he grew a foot taller." Or, "The police are looking for a man with one leg named Smith." Paraphrasing this statement from a newspaper story makes clear the true meaning: "The police are looking for a man named Smith who has one leg."

- *Brainstorming.* Brainstorming is a valuable tool for problem solving, especially when working on humor caused by ambiguity. This technique promotes the active involvement of each individual when working with a group. Encourage ongoing discussion about the items.

- *Vocabulary.* Problems in understanding the vocabulary can adversely affect an individual's performance. Discuss definitions of words that are problematic as they occur.

- *Context clues.* For all types of ambiguity, remind individuals that the interpretation of an item often is dependent upon the context in which it is embedded. Always look for any linguistic and nonlinguistic context clues that may be available. Not every item has context clues.

- *Visual clues.* For visual items, such as cartoons, comic strips, and advertisements, help individuals explore clues such as story situation, setting, facial expressions, gestures, eye gaze, body position, and so forth that may help decipher the ambiguity. Not all visual items have context clues.

- *World knowledge.* Help individuals consider world knowledge factors such as the intention of the speaker, prior utterances, the setting, and the situation described when trying to analyze ambiguous material.

- *Written and oral presentation.* Alert individuals to differences between written and oral presentation for the items. This is especially important for multiple meaning words with spelling differences. For example, the words *knot* and *not* sound the same, but the difference in their meaning can be discerned by seeing how they are spelled.

- *Emphasizing the appropriate word(s).* If an individual has difficulty with a written item after it has been read aloud, reread it with emphasis on the appropriate word or words. If the individual still does not detect the ambiguity, provide it and discuss the two meanings.

- *Contrasting literal and figurative meanings.* For cartoons and comic strips that depict the literal interpretation of a dual-meaning phrase, help individuals grasp the figurative interpretation. It is seeing the contrast between the literal and figurative meanings that makes the item humorous.

- *Referencing texts.* Make use of idiom and proverb dictionaries and thesauri. Appendix D contains a list of suggested texts.

SPECIAL CONSIDERATIONS

Individuals from unique populations may have difficulties that require special attention when dealing with ambiguous language. For example:

- Individuals who have incurred brain injury may need items read several times because of impaired memory skills, or they may have difficulty responding because of impaired sensorimotor speech skills.

- Individuals with impaired hearing may need the support of sign language, emphasis on stress and intonation cues, or greater reliance on nonlinguistic cues (such as facial expressions, gestures, body language, and so forth).

- Individuals who speak English as a second language or who come from linguistically diverse cultural backgrounds may need to have differences between the languages (or dialects) pointed out when interpreting ambiguous utterances. A word or phrase in one language may have a totally different meaning in another. For the goals set forth in this book, the interpretation that is appropriate in standard English should be stressed.

Appendix A provides further information about these and other populations who need to improve their understanding and use of ambiguous language.

ANSWER KEYS

An answer key can be found at the end of each chapter containing intervention items. Although a protocol of correct responses is provided for the stimulus items in each chapter, judging correctness of individuals' responses is left to the discretion of the facilitator.

GLOSSARY

A glossary is provided at the end of the book. This serves as a resource for facilitators when defining terms related to ambiguous language.

OTHER RESOURCES THAT CONTAIN AMBIGUOUS MATERIAL

In addition to materials found in *Saying One Thing, Meaning Another,* in the media, in joke and riddle texts, in conversations, and so forth, several commercially developed intervention products provide ambiguous material for analysis. Note the following:

Cartoon Cut-ups (Hamersky, 1995)

Figurative Language (Gorman-Gard, 1992)

In Plain English (Swiecki and Marston, 1991) (Game format)

Just for Laughs (Spector, 1993) (Game format)

Making Conversation Idiomatic (De Feo, Grimm, and Paige, 1988)

150 Skill-building Reference Lists: Language Remediation and Expansion (Bush, 1989)

Words, Expressions, Contexts (Wiig, 1985)

Workbook for Reasoning Skills (Brubaker, 1983)

3

Reporter:
"Mr. Fields, what do you think about clubs for children?"

W.C. Fields:
"Only when kindness fails."

WORDS WITH MULTIPLE MEANINGS

CHAPTER GOAL

To improve an individual's understanding and use of multiple meaning words

TYPES OF AMBIGUITY

This chapter includes activities for two types of words with multiple meanings (homonyms).

HOMOGRAPHS

A *homograph* is a word that sounds the same and is spelled the same as another word but has a different meaning.
Example: "She has three boyfriends named William. She's a *Bill* collector."

HOMOPHONES

A *homophone* is a word that sounds the same as another word but has a different meaning and a different spelling.
Example: "King Arthur ran the first *knight* school."

TYPES OF ACTIVITIES PROVIDED

The activities in this chapter allow individuals to examine multiple meaning words embedded in story paragraphs, jokes, riddles, signs, cartoons, and comic strips in the following ways:

- using context clues to determine word meaning;
- determining two meanings for highlighted homographs;
- detecting the ambiguous word and providing two meanings for homographs;
- determining two meanings for highlighted homophones;
- detecting the ambiguous word and providing two meanings for homophones; and
- matching the meaning of homophones with their definitions.

BACKGROUND INFORMATION

- Multiple meaning words are ubiquitous in the language heard in social, academic, and work settings, as well as in written language.

- Of the four types of linguistic ambiguity, words with multiple meanings appear to be the easiest to understand (Nippold, 1988; Spector, 1990). Somewhat more difficult are sentences with two meanings, then phrases with multiple meanings such as idiomatic expressions, and, most difficult, ambiguities caused by changes in stress and juncture (Spector, 1990).

- Children have the metalinguistic awareness to resolve ambiguities involving multiple meaning words when they reach the stage of cognitive development Piaget called *concrete operational thinking*. This occurs between 6 and 10 years of age. It is the first type of ambiguity that children learn to resolve (Wallach and Miller, 1988).

- Contextual support available for interpreting multiple meaning words differs. At times, the context offers support for more than one interpretation of the word. Consider, for example, the following riddle: "How are an outfielder and a spider alike? They both catch flies." The words *outfielder* and *spider* bring both definitions of the word *flies* readily to mind. However, in the example, "What did one calculator say to the other calculator? You can count on me," only the literal interpretation is supported by the word *calculator*. The individual would have to know from stored knowledge of vocabulary that *count* also can mean *depend*.

- Individuals must understand and manipulate words with multiple meanings before they can truly understand other types of figurative language such as idioms and proverbs (Wiig and Semel, 1984).

USING CONTEXT CLUES TO DETERMINE WORD MEANING

DIRECTIONS

Some words have two or more different meanings. You can figure out wh[ich] is appropriate by using clues offered in the context in which the word is [used]. [Each] of the following items has questions about the meaning of the italicized word and the clues in the sentence that help to determine its meaning. Answer the questions that follow each item below. Discuss your answers with others.

1a. The leaves of my favorite tree looked like Swiss cheese after the insects got through *boring* holes in them.

   What does *boring* mean in this comment? _____

   _____

   Which clues can be found in the context? _____

   _____

b. I could not stop yawning at the lecture on bird watching last night. It's not a subject I have ever cared about. It was so *boring!*

   What does *boring* mean in this comment? _____

   _____

   Which clues can be found in the context? _____

   _____

2a. Sharon is well dressed, has good manners, and always says the right thing. She sets an excellent example for the other girls to follow. Sharon has *class.*

   What does *class* mean in this comment? _____

   _____

   Which clues can be found in the context? _____

   _____

b. Rita and I see each other every school day. We are in the same history *class.*

   What does *class* mean in this comment? _____

   _____

   Which clues can be found in the context? _____

   _____

Chapter 3 © 1997 CC Spector. Published by Super Duper® Publications.
Duplication permitted for educational use only.

USING CONTEXT CLUES: RUN

DIRECTIONS

Ten meanings for the word *run* are listed below. Use context clues to find the appropriate meaning for each of the items that follow. Answer the questions that follow each item.

A. to go rapidly or hurriedly
B. to ravel lengthwise
C. a regular course of travel
D. to flow rapidly or under pressure
E. to occur persistently
F. to function, operate
G. to spread, dissolve
H. to enter into an election contest
I. a score made in baseball by a runner reaching home plate safely
J. to manage, conduct

1. Stephanie believed she could make a difference in the world if she pursued a political career. She decided to *run* for mayor.

    a. What does *run* mean here? _____
    b. Which clues can be found in the context? _____
    _____

2. You'd better be careful. If you let the water *run* too long, the bathtub will overflow.

    a. What does *run* mean here? _____
    b. Which clues can be found in the context? _____
    _____

3. My dad insists on using the best quality motor oil. He believes it's the only way to be sure your car's engine will *run* properly.

    a. What does *run* mean here? _____
    b. Which clues can be found in the context? _____
    _____

4. Pierre has worked for the railroad for more than 10 years. Now he has the best route of all. He is the conductor on the Paris-to-Marseilles *run*.

    a. What does *run* mean here? _____
    b. Which clues can be found in the context? _____
    _____

Saying One Thing, Meaning Another © 1997 CC Spector. Published by Super Duper® Publications. Duplication permitted for educational use only.

USING CONTEXT CLUES: *RUN*

5. Yitzak's father and grandfather were both excellent violin players. Yitzak started playing the violin when he was three years old. By the time he was five he played beautifully. Musical talent seems to *run* in his family.

   a. What does *run* mean here? _____
   b. Which clues can be found in the context? _____
   _____

6. We need six more dinner rolls. If you *run*, you can get to the bakery before it closes.

   a. What does *run* mean here? _____
   b. Which clues can be found in the context? _____
   _____

7. These stockings were guaranteed not to *run*. I must have caught the fabric on the rough edge of this chair.

   a. What does *run* mean here? _____
   b. Which clues can be found in the context? _____
   _____

8. Oscar put his red shirt in the washing machine with the rest of the clothing. Everything turned pink! He should have known the color would *run*.

   a. What does *run* mean here? _____
   b. Which clues can be found in the context? _____
   _____

9. It's difficult for any boss to *run* a factory when the workers are not willing to follow company rules.

   a. What does *run* mean here? _____
   b. Which clues can be found in the context? _____
   _____

10. Albert was very nervous. If he made this *run*, his team would win the pennant.

    a. What does *run* mean here? _____
    b. Which clues can be found in the context? _____
    _____

USING CONTEXT CLUES: SLIP

DIRECTIONS

Ten meanings for the word *slip* are listed below. Use context clues to find the appropriate meaning for each of the items that follow. Answer the questions that follow each item.

A. to escape from memory or consciousness
B. to say inadvertently
C. to fall from some previous level or standard
D. a mistake in judgment
E. to move quietly and cautiously
F. to slide on a slippery surface
G. a small shoot or twig for planting
H. a boat's berth between two piers, a place to moor a boat
I. to get speedily into or out of clothing
J. an undergarment made to be worn under a dress or skirt

1. Roy came home two hours after his curfew. He tried to *slip* into the house without waking his parents, but they were up waiting for him.

    a. What does *slip* mean here? _____

    b. Which clues can be found in the context? _____
    _____

2. I can't think of the name of the author who wrote that book. Things always seem to *slip* my mind just when I need to know.

    a. What does *slip* mean here? _____

    b. Which clues can be found in the context? _____
    _____

3. I'm afraid I accidentally told JoAnn about the surprise party. It was just a *slip* of the tongue.

    a. What does *slip* mean here? _____

    b. Which clues can be found in the context? _____
    _____

4. We were sailing for hours before we remembered our dinner plans with the Edwardses. It was fortunate that the wind picked up and we were able to make it back to our *slip* very quickly and tie up the boat. We ran down the dock and into the restaurant just in time!

    a. What does *slip* mean here? _____

    b. Which clues can be found in the context? _____
    _____

Saying One Thing, Meaning Another © 1997 CC Spector. Published by Super Duper® Publications. Duplication permitted for educational use only.

USING CONTEXT CLUES: SLIP

5. I've had my rugs cleaned by Bart's Rug Cleaners for years without a problem. This time they don't look really clean. This *slip* in quality just lost them a customer!

   a. What does *slip* mean here? _____

   b. Which clues can be found in the context? _____
   _____

6. Maria thought she could finish the report before the end of the workday. What a *slip*. She still hadn't finished and it was already past quitting time.

   a. What does *slip* mean here? _____

   b. Which clues can be found in the context? _____
   _____

7. My Dad is giving us a *slip* of his prize rosebush. Now we can start growing beautiful roses in our backyard.

   a. What does *slip* mean here? _____

   b. Which clues can be found in the context? _____
   _____

8. After eating that huge dinner, Lorna's clothing felt tight. She couldn't wait to get home so she could *slip* into something more comfortable.

   a. What does *slip* mean here? _____

   b. Which clues can be found in the context? _____
   _____

9. The fabric of Jan's dress was so sheer you could see her underwear right through it. She should have worn a *slip*.

   a. What does *slip* mean here? _____

   b. Which clues can be found in the context? _____
   _____

10. The ice from yesterday's storm covered the driveway and caused my brother to *slip* and hurt his back.

    a. What does *slip* mean here? _____

    b. Which clues can be found in the context? _____
    _____

Chapter 3 © 1997 CC Spector. Published by Super Duper® Publications.
Duplication permitted for educational use only.

MULTIPLE MEANINGS IN WRITTEN PARAGRAPHS

DIRECTIONS

1. Use a dictionary to find words that have at least three meanings (e.g., *draw, hold, line, make, part, plain, point*).

2. Using one or more of these words, make up a story paragraph to support each of the meanings.

3. Discuss the clues offered in the story paragraph that support the appropriate meanings.

STORY PARAGRAPH

CLUES TO MEANINGS

HIGHLIGHTED HOMOGRAPHS

DID YOU KNOW...

A *homograph* is a word that sounds the same and is spelled the same as another word but has a different meaning.

DIRECTIONS

Each item in the homograph activities contains a word (homograph) that is highlighted (bold-faced). Figure out each way the homograph is being used. Look for clues that can help you determine either meaning of the word. A clue can be in any part of the item. If the word is in a cartoon or comic strip, examine the pictures closely for clues for one or both of the meanings. Complete the examples below with someone. Then answer the questions on the activity pages that follow.

- Jack: "Why did Humpty Dumpty have a great **fall**?"
  Jill: "Probably to make up for a rotten summer."

  a. What did Jack mean by *fall*? _____

  b. What did Jill take it to mean? _____

  c. Which words in this joke give you clues to the two meanings?
  _____

- Q: What did the duck say when it finished shopping?
  A: "Just put it on my **bill**."

  a. What did the duck mean? _____

  b. What else could *bill* have meant? _____

  c. Which word in the question gives you the best clue to the second meaning?
  _____

HIGHLIGHTED HOMOGRAPHS

1. Q: What did one math book say to the other math book?
   A: "Boy, do I have **problems**!"

   a. What does the word *problems* mean in this joke? _____

   b. What else can it mean? _____

   c. Which words in the question give you a clue? _____
   _____

2. Q: How can you stop an elephant from **charging**?
   A: Take away his credit cards.

   a. What does *charging* mean in the question? _____

   b. What does it mean in the answer? _____

   c. Which words in the answer give you a clue? _____
   _____

3. Rachel: "I'd like two lamb chops, please, and make them **lean**."
   Butcher: "Certainly, ma'am. Which way?"

   a. What did Rachel mean when she said *lean*? _____

   b. What did the butcher take it to mean? _____

   c. Which words give you a clue to Rachel's meaning? _____
   _____

   d. Which words give you a clue to the butcher's meaning? _____
   _____

4. David: "How did you like that new restaurant on the moon?"
   Sarah: "The food is great, but it just doesn't have any **atmosphere**."

   a. What did Sarah mean by *atmosphere*? _____

   b. What else could it mean? _____

   c. Which word in David's question gives you a clue to the second meaning?
   _____

5. Q: Is it difficult to milk a cow?
   A: No. Any **jerk** can do it.

   a. What does *jerk* mean in the answer? _____

   b. What else can it mean? _____

   c. Which words in the question give you a clue to the second meaning?
   _____

HIGHLIGHTED HOMOGRAPHS

6. Mia: "How did you **come** to fall through the ice?"
   Pia: "I didn't come to fall. I came to skate."

   a. What did Mia mean when she said "*come* to fall through the ice"?
   _____

   b. What did Pia mean when she said *come*? _____
   _____

   c. Which words in Pia's response give you a clue to her meaning?
   _____

7. Look at the cartoon.

   a. What are the two meanings of the word *march* in this cartoon?
   _____

   b. Which word in the cartoon gives you a clue for one of the meanings?
   _____

   c. What do you see in the cartoon that gives you a clue to the other meaning?
   _____

45 | Chapter 3

HIGHLIGHTED HOMOGRAPHS

8. "My uncle tells people he's a **diamond** cutter. He mows the lawn at the baseball stadium."

   a. What does the uncle want people to think when he says *diamond?*
   _____

   b. What does *diamond* really mean in this joke? _____
   _____

   c. Which words give you a clue to the meaning in this joke? _____
   _____

9. "Time **flies like** an arrow. Fruit **flies like** a banana."

   a. How are the words *flies* and *like* being used in the first part of this comment?
   _____
   _____

   b. How are the words *flies* and *like* being used in the second part of the comment? _____
   _____

   c. Which words give you clues? _____
   _____

10. Highway safety billboard:

    > IF YOU LOVE
    > YOUR KID,
    > **BELT** HIM!

    a. What does the word *belt* mean in this sign? _____

    b. What else can it mean? _____
    _____

    c. Which word gives you a clue to the billboard's meaning? _____
    _____

Saying One Thing, Meaning Another © 1997 CC Spector. Published by Super Duper® Publications. Duplication permitted for educational use only.

HOMOGRAPHS

DIRECTIONS

Each item in this section can be taken in two ways because it contains a word that has more than one meaning. Find the word and figure out each way it is being used. Look for clues that can help you determine either meaning of the word. The clue can be in any part of the item. If the word is in a cartoon or comic strip, examine the pictures closely for clues for one or both of the meanings. Complete the examples below with someone. Then answer the questions on the activity pages that follow.

- Beth: "I understand that a dog wears more in the summer than it does in the winter. How is this possible?"

  Michelle: "In the winter, a dog wears a fur coat. In the summer, the same dog wears a fur coat and pants."

  a. Where is the word with more than one meaning found, in Beth's question or in Michelle's answer?_____

  b. Which word can be used in two ways? _____

  c. What does it mean here? _____

  d. What else could it mean? _____

  e. Which word gives you a clue to the second meaning?
  _____

- Sign in the window of a dry-cleaning store:

  Thirty-eight Years on the Same Spot!

  a. Which word in this sign can be taken in two ways?_____
  _____

  b. What are the two meanings? _____
  _____

  c. Which phrase gives you a clue to one of the meanings? _____
  _____

Chapter 3

HOMOGRAPHS I

1. Q. Why do waiters make good tennis players?
   A. They are good at serving.

   a. Which word in the answer can be taken in two ways? _____

   b. What does it mean here? _____

   c. What else can it mean? _____

   d. Which words in the question give you clues to both meanings?
   _____

2. Sign in a dentist's office:

   > **We Are Patient People**

   a. Which word in this sign can be used in two ways? _____

   b. What are the two meanings? _____
   _____

   c. Which word gives you a clue to one of the meanings? _____
   _____

3. Barry: "These drops make my eyes smart."
   Carrie: "Quick—rub some on your head."

   a. Which word in Barry's comment can be used in two ways?
   _____

   b. What did Barry mean? _____

   c. What did Carrie take it to mean? _____

   d. Which words give you a clue to Carrie's meaning? _____
   _____

4. Ted: "Guess what? Golfers aren't using clubs any longer."
   Fred: "They aren't? Why not?"
   Ted: "Because they're long enough now."

   a. Which words in Ted's first comment can be used in two ways?
   _____

   b. What did Ted mean? _____

   c. What did Fred take it to mean? _____
   _____

   d. Which words in Ted's second comment give you a clue to his meaning?
   _____

HOMOGRAPHS I

5. Look at the cartoon.

a. Which word in this cartoon can be used in two ways?
_____

b. What does it mean here? _____
_____

c. What else can it mean? _____
_____

d. Which word in the cartoon gives you a clue to the second meaning?
_____

e. What do you see in the cartoon that gives you clues to both meanings? _____
_____

6. Sign in the window of a delicatessen:

> **If you feel like a coward,
> drop in and we'll make you a hero.**

a. Which word in this sign can be used in two ways?_____

b. What does it mean here? _____

c. What else can it mean?_____

d. Which word in the sign gives you a clue to the second meaning?
_____

7. Jane: "I have the feeling you don't care for our new neighbors."
John: "Not at all. They're the perfect couple. She's a hypochondriac and he's a pill."

a. Which word in John's reply can be used in two ways?_____

b. Which meaning is John using? _____

c. What else can it mean?_____

d. Which word in John's answer gives you a clue to the second meaning?
_____

HOMOGRAPHS I

8. Donald: "My mother knit three socks for my brother in the army."
   Daisy: "Why three socks?"
   Donald: "He wrote and said he had grown another foot."

   a. Which word in Donald's answer to Daisy can be used in two ways?
   _____

   b. What did Donald's mother think it meant?_____
   _____

   c. What did the brother really mean? _____

   d. Which words in Donald's last comment give you a clue to the brother's meaning?_____

9. Q. Why is an empty purse always the same?
   A. Because there is no change in it.

   a. Which word in the answer can be taken in two ways? _____
   _____

   b. What does it mean here? _____

   c. What else can it mean? _____

   d. Which words in the question give you clues to each meaning?
   _____

10. Q. What did the robot say to the magnet?
    A. "I find you very attractive."

    a. Which word in the answer is being used in two ways? _____
    _____

    b. What are the two different meanings? _____
    _____

    c. Which words in the question give you clues to one of the meanings?
    _____
    _____

Saying One Thing, Meaning Another   © 1997 CC Spector. Published by Super Duper® Publications.
                                        Duplication permitted for educational use only.

HOMOGRAPHS II

1. "It's not the minutes spent at the table that put on weight. It's the seconds."

   a. Which word in this joke can be used in two ways? _____

   b. How is it being used here? _____

   c. What else could it mean? _____
   _____

   d. Which words give you a clue to each meaning? _____
   _____

2. Q. What do you call a woman who has three boyfriends named William?
   A. A Bill collector.

   a. Which word in the answer can be used in two ways?
   _____

   b. What does it mean here? _____
   _____

   c. What else can it mean? _____
   _____
   _____

   d. Which word in the question gives you a clue to the first meaning? _____
   _____

   e. What do you see in the cartoon that gives you a clue to the first meaning?
   _____

3. Q. Should you take a waiter along on a canoe trip?
   A. No, because he'll think tipping is allowed.

   a. Which word in the answer can be used in two ways? _____
   _____

   b. What does it mean here? _____

   c. What else can it mean? _____

   d. Which words in the question give you a clue to each meaning?
   _____

HOMOGRAPHS II

4. Reporter: "Mr. Marx, what do you think of women's rights?"
   Groucho Marx: "I like either side of them."

   a. Which word can be used in two ways? _____

   b. What did the reporter mean? _____
   _____

   c. What did Groucho mean? _____
   _____

   d. What is it about each of the speakers in this exchange that gives you clues to their meanings? _____
   _____

5. Look at the cartoon.

SALLY WAS PUZZLED WHEN SHE CAME UPON A FORK IN THE ROAD.

   a. Which word in this cartoon caption is being used in two ways? _____
   _____

   b. What does it mean here? _____
   _____
   _____

   c. What else can it mean? _____
   _____
   _____

   d. What do you see in the cartoon that gives you a clue to each meaning? _____
   _____

6. José: "How do you make a hamburger roll?"
   Juanita: "Take it to the top of a hill and give it a shove."

   a. Which word is being used in two ways? _____

   b. What do you think José meant? _____
   _____

   c. What did Juanita think he meant? _____
   _____

   d. Which words in Juanita's response give you a clue to what she thought?
   _____

Saying One Thing, Meaning Another © 1997 CC Spector. Published by Super Duper® Publications. Duplication permitted for educational use only.

HOMOGRAPHS II

7. Look at the cartoon.

MILLIONS OF YEARS AGO DINOSAURS RULED THE EARTH.

a. Which word in this cartoon caption is being used in two ways? _____

b. What does it mean here? _____
_____
_____

c. What else can it mean? _____
_____
_____

d. What do you see in the cartoon that gives you a clue to the first meaning? _____
_____
_____

8. Q. An orange and a lemon were on a high diving board. The orange jumped off. Why didn't the lemon?
   A. Because it was yellow.

   a. Which word in the answer can be used in two ways? _____

   b. What does it mean here? _____

   c. What else can it mean? _____

   d. Which words in the question give you a clue to the first meaning?
   _____

9. Lou: "Whatever happened to that bowlegged cowboy we knew?"
   Bud: "He lost his job. Seems he couldn't keep his calves together."

   a. Which word in Bud's answer can have two meanings? _____

   b. What are the two meanings? _____
   _____

   c. Which words in Lou's question give you the best clues for each meaning?
   _____

53 | Chapter 3

© 1997 CC Spector. Published by Super Duper® Publications.
Duplication permitted for educational use only.

HOMOGRAPHS II

10. Look at the cartoon.

NOAH: "OKAY, ALL OF YOU ANIMALS, GO FORTH AND MULTIPLY."
SNAKES: "NOT US."
NOAH: "AND WHY NOT?"
SNAKES: "WE'RE ADDERS."

a. Which word in this joke can be taken in two ways? _____

b. What does it mean here? _____

c. What else can it mean? _____

d. Which word in the joke gives you a clue to the second meaning? _____

e. What do you see in the cartoon that gives you a clue to the first meaning? _____

11. Q. What do ducks call their community?
    A. Down town.

a. Which word in the answer can be used in two ways? _____

b. What does it mean here? _____

c. What else can it mean? _____

d. Which word in the question gives you a clue to the first meaning? _____

54 Saying One Thing, Meaning Another   © 1997 CC Spector. Published by Super Duper® Publications. Duplication permitted for educational use only.

HOMOGRAPHS III

1. Q. Why did the teacher come to school wearing sunglasses?
   A. Because her class was so bright.

   a. Which word in the answer can be used in two ways? _____

   b. What does it mean here? _____
   _____

   c. What else can it mean? _____

   d. Which word in the question gives you a clue to the first meaning?
   _____

2. Q. Where did the mayor keep money for snow removal?
   A. In a slush fund.

   a. Which word in the answer can be used in two ways? _____

   b. What does it mean here? _____
   _____

   c. What else can it mean? _____
   _____

   d. Which words in the question give you a clue to the first meaning?
   _____

3. Bumper sticker:

   Minds are like parachutes.
   They function only when they are opened.

   a. Which word in this bumper sticker can be used in two ways?
   _____

   b. What are the two meanings? _____
   _____
   _____

   c. Which words give you a clue to each meaning? _____
   _____

HOMOGRAPHS III

4. Hotel: A place where you trade dollars for quarters.

   a. Which word in this "definition" can be used in two ways?
   _____

   b. What are the two meanings? _____
   _____

   c. Which words give you a clue to each meaning? _____
   _____

5. Patient: "I feel funny today. What should I do?"
   Doctor: "Become a comedian."

   a. Which word in the patient's comment can be used in two ways?
   _____

   b. What did the patient mean? _____

   c. What did the doctor take it to mean? _____

   d. Which words in this joke give you a clue to each meaning? _____
   _____

6. Father: "Money doesn't grow on trees, you know!"
   Son: "Then why does the bank have so many branches?"

   a. Which word in the son's question can be used in two ways? _____
   _____

   b. What does the son mean? _____

   c. What else can it mean? _____

   d. Which word in the father's comment gives you a clue to the second meaning?
   _____

7. Sue: "Watch out for Tex over there. He's a cowboy artist."
   Tom: "You mean he specializes in western scenes?"
   Sue: "No, he's always drawing a gun."

   a. Which word in this joke can be taken in two ways? _____

   b. What does Tom think it means? _____

   c. What does Sue mean? _____

   d. Which word in Sue's first comment gives you a clue to her meaning?
   _____

Saying One Thing, Meaning Another

HOMOGRAPHS III

8. Q. How are an engaged girl and a telephone alike?
   A. They both have rings.

   a. Which word in the answer is being used in two ways? _____
   _____

   b. What are the two meanings? _____
   _____

   c. Which words in the question give you clues to each meaning?
   _____

9. Q. How are baseball and baking alike?
   A. In both, you need a good batter to make dough.

   a. Which words in the answer can be used in two ways? _____
   _____

   b. What are the two meanings of the first word? _____
   _____
   _____

   c. What are the two meanings of the second word? _____
   _____
   _____

   d. Which words in the question give you clues to each word's two meanings?
   _____
   _____

10. Headline in a pet magazine:

    "KITTEN WINS MILK-DRINKING CONTEST BY THREE LAPS!"

    a. Which word in this "headline" can be used in two ways? _____
    _____

    b. What does it mean here? _____
    _____

    c. What else can it mean? _____

    d. Which words give you a clue to the first meaning? _____
    _____

STORY PARAGRAPH CONTAINING HOMOGRAPHS

DIRECTIONS

Underline the words in the following paragraph that can be used in more than one way. Tell what each of the words you have underlined means in this story. If desired, use the space at the bottom of this page to list the homographs and their meanings.

The police car screamed in from Maple Street. Officer Dennis lit out of the car and jumped the fleeing suspect. He kept him covered until Jones arrived. Two men were down. "I'll watch this guy, you call an ambulance," Dennis said to Jones. The fact that Dennis nailed this guy so quickly was going to look great on his record.

HOMOGRAPH   **MEANING**

Saying One Thing, Meaning Another

WORDS AND THEIR MEANINGS

DIRECTIONS

Many common words have different meanings in computer language. Match each of the following words to its computer-related meaning. Then answer the questions in item 8.

1. mouse _____
2. window _____
3. bit _____
4. menu _____
5. virus _____
6. path _____
7. bug _____

A. a separate viewing area on a computer display screen

B. programs or other choices displayed on the monitor for user selection

C. a device to move a pointer on a screen

D. smallest piece of information a computer can process

E. a mistake that occurs in a program within a computer or in the unit's electrical system

F. route by which computer programs move between areas in the computer to get data or instructions

G. hidden computer code designed to destroy information

8a. What is the meaning of *computer virus* as it relates to the cartoon? _____
_____
_____
_____

b. What clues do you see that support this meaning?
_____
_____
_____
_____

HIGHLIGHTED HOMOPHONES

DID YOU KNOW...

A *homophone* is a word that sounds the same as another word but has a different meaning and a different spelling.

DIRECTIONS

Each item in this section contains a homophone that is highlighted (bold-faced). The questions after each item will ask you to do the following:

- determine the meaning of the highlighted word;
- figure out the alternate spelling; and
- determine the meaning of the word with the new spelling.

Look for clues that lead to the word's meaning for each way it is spelled. The clue can be in any part of the item. If the word is in a cartoon or comic strip, examine the pictures closely for clues for one or both of the meanings. Complete the examples below with someone. Then answer the questions on the activity pages that follow.

- Mia: Did all the animals on Noah's ark come in **pairs**?
  Lee: No, the worms came in apples.

  a. What does the highlighted word mean? _____

  b. How else can the highlighted word be spelled? _____

  c. What does it mean with the new spelling? _____

  d. Which word in Lee's answer gives you a clue to the new meaning?
  _____

- Q. What happens when you park a frog illegally?
  A. You get **toad** away.

  a. What does the highlighted word mean? _____

  b. How else can the highlighted word be spelled? _____

  c. What does it mean with the new spelling? _____

  d. Which words in the question give you a clue to the new meaning?
  _____

60 | Saying One Thing, Meaning Another © 1997 CC Spector. Published by Super Duper® Publications. Duplication permitted for educational use only.

HIGHLIGHTED HOMOPHONES

1. She: "I was in the movie *The Breakfast Club*."
   He: "Really?"
   She: "Sure! I had a big **roll**."

   a. What does the highlighted word mean here? _____

   b. How else can it be spelled? _____

   c. What does it mean with the new spelling? _____
   _____

   d. Which words in the first comment give you a clue to the new meaning?
   _____

2. Look at the cartoon.

   Q. WHAT DO GRAPES DO WHEN PEOPLE STEP ON THEM?

   A. THEY LET OUT A LITTLE **WHINE**.

   a. What does the highlighted word mean?
   _____

   b. How else can the highlighted word be spelled?
   _____
   _____

   c. What does it mean with the new spelling?
   _____
   _____

   d. Which words in the question give you clues to each meaning? _____
   _____
   _____

   e. What do you see in the cartoon that gives you a clue to the first meaning? _____

3. Q. What are the strongest days of the week?
   A. Saturday and Sunday. Monday through Friday are **week**days.

   a. What does the highlighted word mean? _____

   b. How else can the highlighted word be spelled? _____

   c. What does it mean with the new spelling? _____
   _____

   d. Which word in the question gives you a clue to the new meaning? _____
   _____

HIGHLIGHTED HOMOPHONES

4. Teacher: "Who knows where the Great **Plains** are?"
   Student: "At the big airports."

   a. What does the highlighted word mean here? _____
   _____

   b. How else can it be spelled? _____

   c. What does it mean with the new spelling? _____
   _____

   d. Which word in the student's answer gives you a clue to the new meaning?
   _____

5. Look at the cartoon.

   a. What does the highlighted word in the sign mean?
   _____

   b. How else can the highlighted word be spelled?
   _____

   c. What does it mean with the new spelling?
   _____
   _____

   d. Which word in the sign gives you a clue to the new meaning? _____

6. When the housekeeper went to Tokyo for her vacation, she left the following note:

   > Maid
   > *in*
   > *Japan*

   a. What does the highlighted word mean? _____

   b. How else can it be spelled? _____

   c. What does it mean with the new spelling? _____
   _____

   d. Which word in the sign gives you a clue to the new meaning?
   _____

Saying One Thing, Meaning Another   © 1997 CC Spector. Published by Super Duper® Publications.
Duplication permitted for educational use only.

HIGHLIGHTED HOMOPHONES

7. Q. When is a green book no longer green?
   A. When it is **read**.

   a. What does the highlighted word mean? _____

   b. How else can it be spelled? _____

   c. What does it mean with the new spelling? _____

   d. Which word in the question gives you a clue to the new meaning?
   _____

8. Highway safety sign:

   > Be wreckless, not reckless.

   a. What does *wreckless* mean? _____

   b. What does *reckless* mean? _____

   c. Which words give you a clue to the two meanings? _____

9. Name of a store that sells eyeglasses:

   > **FOR** EYES

   a. What does the highlighted word mean? _____

   b. How else can it be spelled? _____

   c. To what does the sign refer if the new spelling is used? _____

   d. Which word gives you a clue to the new meaning?
   _____

HIGHLIGHTED HOMOPHONES

10. Look at the cartoon.

KING ARTHUR WAS THE FIRST TEACHER AT **KNIGHT** SCHOOL.

a. What does the highlighted word mean? _____

b. How else can it be spelled? _____

c. What does it mean with the new spelling? _____
_____

d. What do you see in the cartoon that gives you clues to the new meaning? _____
_____

Saying One Thing, Meaning Another

HIGHLIGHTED WORD STORY

DIRECTIONS
Give each highlighted (bold-faced) word in this story its correct meaning by changing the spelling.

"**Ewe** are always complaining when **eye** say anything
_____   _____

about your driving. Well, give me a **brake**! If **eye**
                                    _____ _____

hadn't **tolled ewe** about that **grate** big **whole** in the
        _____ _____   _____   _____

rode, **ewe wood** have damaged your car, and it **wood**
_____   _____ _____   _____

have had to be **toad**."
               _____

65 | Chapter 3 © 1997 CC Spector. Published by Super Duper® Publications. Duplication permitted for educational use only.

HOMOPHONES

DIRECTIONS

Each item in the homophone activities can be taken in two ways because it contains a word that sounds the same as another word but has a different meaning and a different spelling. The questions after each item will ask you to do the following:

- find the word that can be spelled in two ways;
- figure out what it means as it is used in the item;
- find an alternate spelling;
- determine the meaning of the word with the new spelling; and
- look for clues to the word's meaning for each way it is spelled.

The clue can be in any part of the item. If the word is in a cartoon or comic strip, examine the pictures closely for clues for one or both of the meanings. Complete the examples below with someone. Then answer the questions on the activity pages that follow.

- Q. Why couldn't the church steeple keep a secret?
  A. Because the bell always tolled.

  a. Which word in the answer can be spelled differently to change its meaning?
  _____

  b. What does it mean here? _____

  c. How else can it be spelled? _____

  d. What does it mean with the new spelling? _____
  _____

  e. Which words in the question give you a clue to the new meaning?
  _____

- Lonnie: What happens when 50 rabbits hop backwards at the same time?
  Ezra: You get a receding hare line.

  a. Which word in the answer can be spelled differently to change its meaning?
  _____

  b. What does it mean here? _____

  c. How else can it be spelled? _____

  d. What does it mean with the new spelling? _____
  _____

  e. Which word in Ezra's answer gives you a clue to the new meaning?
  _____

HOMOPHONES 1

1. Chubby husband: "If I don't eat this last piece of cake, it'll go to waste."
   Wife: "And if you do eat it, it'll go to waist."

   a. Which words sound alike in this joke? _____

   b. What does the husband mean? _____
   _____

   c. What does the wife mean? _____
   _____

   d. Which word in the joke gives you a clue to the wife's meaning?
   _____

2. Nelson: "Do you think I should complain about the high price of this airplane ticket?"
   Harriet: "Why complain? It's a fare price."

   a. Which word in Harriet's answer can be spelled differently to change its meaning? _____

   b. What does it mean here? _____

   c. How else can it be spelled? _____

   d. What does it mean with the new spelling? _____

   e. Which words in Nelson's question give you a clue to the first meaning?
   _____

3. "I know a man who makes deliveries for a foot doctor. He drives the toe truck."

   a. Which word in this joke can be spelled differently to change its meaning? _____

   b. What does it mean here? _____

   c. How else can it be spelled? _____

   d. What does it mean with the new spelling? _____

   e. Which word in the joke gives you a clue to the new meaning? _____
   _____

   f. Which word gives you a clue to the first meaning? _____
   _____

HOMOPHONES I

4. Look at the cartoon.

NURSE: "THE DOCTOR WILL SEE YOU NOW."
PATIENT: "WHICH DOCTOR?"
NURSE: "NO, JUST A REGULAR ONE."

a. Which word in this joke can be spelled differently to change its meaning? _____

b. What does the patient mean here? _____
_____

c. How else can the word be spelled? _____

d. What does it mean with the new spelling? _____
_____
_____

e. What do you see in the cartoon that gives you a clue to the patient's meaning? _____
_____

5. Man in a seafood restaurant: "I'd like a lobster tail."
   Waiter: "Certainly sir. Once upon a time there was this handsome lobster..."

   a. Which word in the man's comment can be spelled differently to change its meaning? _____

   b. What does it mean here? _____

   c. How else can it be spelled? _____

   d. What does it mean with the new spelling? _____
   _____

   e. Which words in the waiter's response give you a clue for the new meaning?
   _____

6. Q. Which animal is richer: a duck or a skunk?
   A. A duck, because it has a bill. A skunk has only a scent.

   a. Which word in the answer can be spelled differently to change its meaning?
   _____

   b. What does it mean here? _____

   c. How else can it be spelled? _____

   d. What does it mean with the new spelling? _____
   _____

HOMOPHONES I

e. Which other word in the answer can be used in two ways? _____

f. What does it mean here? _____

g. What else can it mean? _____
_____

h. Which word in the question gives you a clue to the second meaning of each word? _____

7. Look at the cartoon.

A MAN GOT A BIG INCREASE IN SALARY, SO HE SENT HIS MOTHER ON A VACATION. SHE SPENT TWO WEEKS ON THE BEACH ENJOYING THE SON'S RAISE.

a. Which two words in this joke can be spelled differently to change each word's meaning? _____
_____

b. What do they mean here? _____
_____

c. How else can they be spelled? _____
_____

d. What do they mean with the new spelling? _____
_____

e. What do you see in the cartoon that gives you a clue to the new meaning? _____
_____

8. Mama fish: "Don't bite that hook!"
Baby fish: "Why not?"
Mama fish: "You're too young to face the reel world."

a. Which word in Mama's reply can be spelled differently to change its meaning? _____
_____

b. What does it mean here? _____

c. How else can it be spelled? _____

d. What does it mean with the new spelling? _____
_____

e. Which words in Mama's opening statement give you a clue to the first meaning? _____

HOMOPHONES I

9. Q. Why did Zorro have so many sword fights?
   A. He was leading a duel life.

   a. Which word in the answer can be spelled differently to change its meaning?
   _____

   b. What does it mean here? _____

   c. How else can it be spelled? _____

   d. What does it mean with the new spelling? _____
   _____

   e. Which words in the question give you a clue to the original meaning?
   _____

10. Sign over diet products in a health food store:

   a. Which word in this sign can be spelled differently to change its meaning?
   _____

   b. What does it mean here? _____

   c. How else can it be spelled? _____

   d. What does it mean with the new spelling? _____
   _____

   e. Which words give you a clue to the new meaning? _____
   _____

70 Saying One Thing, Meaning Another   © 1997 CC Spector. Published by Super Duper® Publications.
                                          Duplication permitted for educational use only.

HOMOPHONES II

1. Lance: "I help the carpenter. I pick up tacks."
   Ann: "Oh, you're a tacks collector."

   a. Which word in Ann's comment can be spelled differently to change its meaning? _____

   b. What does it mean here? _____

   c. How else can it be spelled? _____

   d. What does it mean with the new spelling? _____
   _____

   e. Which word in Ann's comment gives you a clue to the second meaning?
   _____

2. Mama hen: "I'm going to wash your beak out with soap."
   Baby chick: "Why, Mama?"
   Mama hen: "Because you used fowl language."

   a. Which word in Mama's answer can be spelled differently to change its meaning?_____

   b. What does it mean here? _____

   c. How else can it be spelled? _____

   d. What does it mean with the new spelling? _____
   _____

   e. Which words in Mama's first comment give you a clue to the second meaning?
   _____

3. Look at the road sign.

   Repair Crew Ahead Give 'em a Brake!

   a. Which word in this sign can be spelled differently to change its meaning?
   _____

   b. What does it mean here? _____
   _____

   c. How else can it be spelled?
   _____

   d. What does it mean with the new spelling? _____
   _____

   e. Which words in the sign give you a clue to the second meaning?
   _____

71 | Chapter 3

HOMOPHONES II

4. Censors: People who stick their "nos" into other people's business.

   a. Which word in this "definition" can be spelled differently to change its meaning? _____

   b. What does it mean here? _____

   c. How else can it be spelled? _____

   d. What does it mean with the new spelling? _____
   _____

   e. Which word gives you a clue to the first meaning? _____
   _____

5. New dad showing a guest his home: "And this is the way to the bawl room."

   a. Which word in the dad's comment can be spelled differently to change its meaning? _____

   b. What does it mean here? _____

   c. How else can it be spelled? _____

   d. What does it mean with the new spelling? _____
   _____

   e. Which words give you a clue to the first meaning? _____
   _____

6. Q. Why are bakers foolish people?
   A. Because they always sell what they knead.

   a. Which word in the answer can be spelled differently to change its meaning?
   _____

   b. What does it mean here? _____

   c. How else can it be spelled? _____

   d. What does it mean with the new spelling? _____
   _____

   e. Which word gives you a clue to the second meaning? _____
   _____

Saying One Thing, Meaning Another © 1997 CC Spector. Published by Super Duper® Publications. Duplication permitted for educational use only.

HOMOPHONES II

7. Surita: "Did you hear about the glassblower who accidentally inhaled?"
   Colita: "No, what happened?"
   Surita: "He got a pane in his stomach."

   a. Which word in Surita's response can be spelled differently to change its meaning? _____

   b. What does it mean here? _____

   c. How else can it be spelled? _____

   d. What does it mean with the new spelling? _____

   e. Which word in Surita's question gives you a clue to the first meaning?
   _____

8. "The first time I ever had gum was on a chew-chew train."

   a. Which word can be spelled differently to change its meaning?
   _____

   b. What does it mean here? _____

   c. How else can it be spelled? _____

   d. What does it mean with the new spelling? _____
   _____

   e. Which words in this joke give you a clue to each meaning?
   _____

9. Q. Why couldn't the colt talk?
   A. He was a little hoarse.

   a. Which word in the answer can be spelled differently to change its meaning?
   _____

   b. What does it mean here? _____

   c. How else can it be spelled? _____

   d. What does it mean with the new spelling? _____
   _____

   e. Which words in the question give you a clue to each meaning? _____
   _____

HOMOPHONES II

10. Q. Why is your nose in the middle of your face?
    A. Because it's the scenter.

    a. Which word in the answer can be spelled differently to change its meaning?
    _____

    b. What does it mean here? _____

    c. How else can it be spelled? _____

    d. What does it mean with the new spelling? _____
    _____

    e. Which words in the question give you a clue to the second meaning?
    _____
    _____

HOMOPHONES III

1. Q. Do you know what an obituary reporter does?
   A. Last writes.

   a. Which word in the answer can be spelled differently to change its meaning?
   _____

   b. What does it mean here? _____

   c. How else can it be spelled? _____

   d. What does it mean with the new spelling? _____
   _____

   e. Which word in the question gives you a clue to the second meaning?
   _____

2. Q. What dog has money?
   A. A bloodhound, because it is always picking up scents.

   a. Which word in the answer can be spelled differently to change its meaning?
   _____

   b. What does it mean here? _____

   c. How else can it be spelled? _____

   d. What does it mean with the new spelling? _____
   _____

   e. Which word in the question gives you a clue to the second meaning?
   _____

3. Q. Which trees come in twos?
   A. Pear trees.

   a. Which word in the answer can be spelled differently to change its meaning?
   _____

   b. What does it mean here? _____

   c. How else can it be spelled? _____

   d. What does it mean with the new spelling? _____
   _____

   e. Which word in the question gives you a clue to the second meaning?
   _____

Chapter 3

© 1997 CC Spector. Published by Super Duper® Publications.
Duplication permitted for educational use only.

HOMOPHONES III

4. Q. What did the penmanship teacher say to Orville?
   A. Write right, Wright.

   What does each of the words in the answer mean?

   _____
   _____
   _____

5. Q. If money could smell, why would you use pennies to detect odors?

   A. Because cents sense scents.

   What does each of the last three words in the answer mean?

   _____
   _____
   _____

6. Several girls ran in the race, but only one won.

   What do the last two words of this comment mean?

   _____
   _____

7. Q. How can you tell if food is spoiled?
   A. The nose knows.

   What do the last two words in the answer mean?

   _____
   _____

8. Q. If you served dinner to four couples, how many people dined?
   A. Eight ate.

   What does each word in the answer mean?

   _____
   _____

HOMOPHONES III

9. Q. What is a baseball stadium filled with when the home team wins the world series?
   A. Tiers of joy.

   a. Which word in the answer can be spelled in two ways? _____
   _____

   b. What does it mean here? _____

   c. How else can it be spelled? _____

   d. What does it mean with the new spelling? _____
   _____

   e. Which words in the question give you a clue to the first meaning?
   _____

10. Sign in a tailor shop:

    > *We'll sew for you. We'll press for you.*
    > *We'll even dye for you.*

    a. Which word in the sign can be spelled differently to change its meaning?
    _____

    b. What does it mean here? _____

    c. How else can it be spelled? _____

    d. What does it mean with the new spelling? _____
    _____

    e. Which words in the sign give you clues to the first meaning? _____
    _____

ADDITIONAL ACTIVITIES

1. Ask the individuals to browse through a dictionary to find words that have multiple meanings. See how many words can be found (in an allotted amount of time) that have more than three meanings. Encourage the individuals to generate as many definitions of each word as possible before checking the dictionary definitions.

2. Ask the individuals to underline or circle all the multiple meaning words they can find in a newspaper article or page of a magazine story. Raise awareness by discussing the frequency with which such words occur. Discuss the meanings of the multiple meaning words underlined or circled as they relate to the context of the reading material.

3. Ask the individuals to examine the sports section of a newspaper. List all the ambiguous words in the headlines and/or articles. Draw attention to the numerous ways of stating that one team was victorious over another team.

4. Ask the individuals to write paragraphs using specified multiple meaning words. Discuss how the words were used within the contexts of their paragraphs.

5. Advise the individuals to write down any multiple meaning words heard in conversations, movies, television shows, etc. that are not understood. Encourage the use of a dictionary to determine the appropriate meanings.

CHAPTER 3 ANSWER KEY

These answers are merely guidelines. The facilitator can judge if the individual's responses are appropriate for each item.

USING CONTEXT CLUES TO DETERMINE WORD MEANING

1a. making holes, piercing leaves

　looked like Swiss cheese, because they are full of holes (insects did something that made holes)

b. dull, uninteresting, tiresome

　could not stop yawning, didn't care for the subject of bird watching

2a. she has elegance, she is a person of high quality

　sets an excellent example to follow, words describing a person with good qualities (well dressed, good manners, always says the right thing)

b. a group of students meeting regularly to study the same subject

　school, history class

USING CONTEXT CLUES: RUN

1a. H
b. political career, mayor

2a. D
b. water, bathtub will overflow

3a. F
b. motor oil, car's engine

4a. C
b. railroad, best route of all, conductor, Paris to Marseilles

5a. E
b. father and grandfather were both excellent violin players, musical talent, in his family

6a. A
b. get to the bakery before it closes

7a. B
b. stockings, caught the fabric on the rough edge of this chair

8a. G
b. red shirt in the washing machine, everything turned pink, color

9a. J
b. boss, factory

10a. I
b. team, win the pennant

CHAPTER 3 ANSWER KEY

USING CONTEXT CLUES: SLIP

1a. E
 b. came home two hours after his curfew, without waking his parents

2a. A
 b. can't think of the name of the author

3a. B
 b. accidentally told JoAnn about the surprise party

4a. H
 b. sailing, tie up the boat, ran down the dock

5a. C
 b. rugs cleaned for years without a problem, this time they don't look really clean

6a. D
 b. thought she could finish, still hadn't finished

7a. G
 b. rosebush, now we can start growing beautiful roses

8a. I
 b. clothing felt tight, couldn't wait (to change clothing)

9a. J
 b. fabric so sheer you could see her underwear

10a. F
 b. ice covered the driveway, hurt his back

HIGHLIGHTED HOMOGRAPHS

Examples:

- a. to drop down from a high place

  b. autumn, a season of the year

  c. Jack and Jill and Humpty Dumpty, because they are nursery rhyme characters (Humpty Dumpty fell off a wall, and Jack and Jill fell down a hill); summer, because it is a season of the year

- a. I won't pay you now, I'm charging the things I've bought; I'll pay for them at a later date.

  b. the duck's beak

  c. duck, because ducks have bills

1a. troubles

 b. mathematical questions

 c. math book

CHAPTER 3 ANSWER KEY

2a. attacking, running at you
  b. deferred payment on an account to be paid at a future time
  c. credit cards

3a. without fat
  b. tilted to one side
  c. lamb chops, because they generally have fat on them
  d. which way

4a. pleasant setting, nice surroundings
  b. air that people can breathe
  c. moon, because there is no breathable air on the moon

5a. fool, incompetent person
  b. pull, tug, yank
  c. milk a cow, because pulling the udders is necessary for getting the milk

6a. happen to fall through the ice
  b. arrive at the ice rink
  c. I came to skate

7a. a month of the year, walking in a rhythmic manner
  b. month
  c. the children walking in a line and playing instruments like a marching band

8a. precious gem
  b. the shape of a baseball field
  c. baseball stadium

9a. moves rapidly, similar to
  b. insects, enjoy
  c. arrow, because it moves very quickly; fruit flies, because they are a type of insect; and banana, because insects are often seen buzzing around fruit

10a. put on his seatbelt
  b. hit him
  c. safety, because we wear seatbelts to keep us safe

HOMOGRAPHS

Examples:

- a. Michelle's answer
  b. pants
  c. an item of clothing
  d. breathing hard
  e. summer, because animals get hot, and that's when they pant

CHAPTER 3
ANSWER KEY

- a. spot
  b. location of the store, a stain or dirt on clothing
  c. dry-cleaning store

HOMOGRAPHS I

1a. serving
  b. putting the ball into play in a tennis game
  c. bringing food and beverages to customers in restaurants
  d. waiters, tennis players

2a. patient
  b. person seen by a dentist to have dental work done, waiting calmly and without complaint
  c. dentist, because dentists have patients

3a. smart
  b. burn, sting
  c. intelligent
  d. rub some on your head

4a. longer, clubs
  b. the length of the club
  c. not using golf clubs anymore, a place where golf is played
  d. long enough, which indicates a measurement

5a. flip
  b. enjoy immensely
  c. turn hamburgers over
  d. burgers, because you turn (flip) them over
  e. the man is holding a tool to turn burgers, and he is happily somersaulting (flipping) over the barbecue grill

6a. hero
  b. a kind of sandwich
  c. a brave person
  d. coward, because it is the opposite of hero

7a. pill
  b. annoying person
  c. dose of medicine
  d. hypochondriac, because people who have hypochondria are overly concerned about their health and may take a lot of medicine

8a. foot
  b. the part of his leg that he stands on
  c. a measurement, 12 inches
  d. he had grown

CHAPTER 3 ANSWER KEY

9a. change
   b. difference
   c. coins, money
   d. empty purse, always the same

10a. attractive
   b. pretty, having personal charm; possessing a physical force that attracts metal
   c. robot, because it is often made out of metal, magnet

HOMOGRAPHS II

1a. seconds
   b. another helping of food
   c. units of time that make up a minute
   d. minutes, because it relates to time; put on weight, because eating too much food can make you fat

2a. Bill
   b. a man's name
   c. monies owed
   d. William, because Bill is a nickname for William
   e. all the men are named Bill

3a. tipping
   b. overturning the canoe, capsizing
   c. gratuity for service
   d. waiter, because they are given tips for service; canoe, because it can tip over very easily

4a. rights
   b. fair and equal treatment socially, economically, legally, etc.
   c. the right side of women's bodies
   d. reporters typically ask politically oriented questions; Groucho Marx, a comedian, would have responded humorously by referring to a different meaning

5a. fork
   b. a utensil for eating
   c. a place in a road that divides into two or more branches
   d. Sally looks puzzled when she sees a fork used for eating lying in the road, and the road she is on divides into two branches, which also may confuse her

6a. roll
   b. a hamburger bun
   c. move along, tumble downhill
   d. top of a hill, give it a shove

CHAPTER 3
ANSWER KEY

7a. ruled
 b. dinosaurs were drawing straight lines with rulers
 c. controlled, governed, were the supreme power
 d. the dinosaurs are using rulers

8a. yellow
 b. cowardly
 c. a color
 d. high diving board, because it takes courage to jump off a high diving board

9a. calves
 b. the fleshy back part of the leg below the knee, the offspring of cows
 c. bowlegged cowboy, because a cowboy works with cows and their offspring (calves); and when one has bowed legs it is not possible to keep the lower part of the legs (calves) together

10a. adders
 b. a type of snake
 c. individual who performs mathematical procedures like addition
 d. multiply, because it is also a mathematical procedure
 e. snakes

11a. down
 b. a covering of soft, fluffy feathers
 c. direction, position
 d. ducks, because they have down

HOMOGRAPHS III

1a. bright
 b. radiating light, shining
 c. intelligent, smart
 d. sunglasses

2a. slush
 b. melted or watery snow
 c. a fund for bribing public officials or carrying on corruptive propaganda
 d. money for snow removal

3a. opened
 b. receptive to arguments or ideas; to move from a closed position
 c. minds, parachutes

4a. quarters
 b. living accommodations, lodgings; a coin worth one-fourth of a dollar
 c. hotel, dollars

CHAPTER 3
ANSWER KEY

5a. funny
 b. different from usual in an unpleasant way
 c. amusing, humorous
 d. patient, doctor, comedian

6a. branches
 b. separate divisions of a main organization
 c. secondary stems coming from the trunk of a tree
 d. trees

7a. drawing
 b. making a picture
 c. pulling out a gun
 d. cowboy, because in movies he frequently has a gun

8a. rings
 b. a piece of jewelry generally worn on a finger; sound made by a telephone
 c. engaged girl, telephone

9a. batter, dough
 b. person at bat in a baseball game; a mixture of flour, liquid, and other ingredients
 c. money; a mixture of flour, liquid, and other ingredients that is stiff enough to knead or roll
 d. baseball, baking

10a. laps
 b. to take in liquid or food with the tongue
 c. circuit around a race course
 d. kitten, milk-drinking contest

STORY PARAGRAPH CONTAINING HOMOGRAPHS

screamed—made a shrill noise

lit—took off in a hurry

jumped—suddenly pounced on

covered—used a weapon to control his movement

down—wounded

watch—see that he doesn't move

call—to use the telephone

nailed—captured

great—very good

record—list of accomplishments

CHAPTER 3
ANSWER KEY

WORDS AND THEIR MEANINGS

1. mouse (C)
2. window (A)
3. bit (D)
4. menu (B)
5. virus (G)
6. path (F)
7. bug (E)
8a. computer is sick (has a virus, or the flu)
  b. the computer looks ill, and may have chills because it is wearing a scarf

HIGHLIGHTED HOMOPHONES

Examples:

- a. two of each kind
  b. pears
  c. a kind of fruit
  d. apples, because, like pears, they are a kind of fruit

- a. tailless, leaping amphibian
  b. towed
  c. pulled along, dragged
  d. park illegally, because to do so would cause you to be towed away

1a. type of bread
  b. role
  c. part played by an actor
  d. was in the movie

2a. a complaining cry
  b. wine
  c. a fermented grape juice, a beverage
  d. grapes, because they are used to make wine; step on them, because it hurts to be stepped on
  e. the grapes appear to be making sounds as if they are hurt

3a. midweek rather than weekend days
  b. weak
  c. having little or no strength
  d. strongest, because strong is the opposite of weak

CHAPTER 3
ANSWER KEY

4a. a broad, unbroken expanse of land
 b. planes
 c. aircraft
 d. airports

5a. an exclamation of pleasure or delight
 b. Oz
 c. the name of a place
 d. Wizard, because *The Wizard of Oz* is a well-known book and movie

6a. housekeeper, female servant
 b. made
 c. manufactured
 d. Japan, a country commonly named on labels of manufactured goods

7a. information has been taken in by someone seeing written letters or symbols that have meaning
 b. red
 c. a color
 d. green, because it also is a color

8a. never having had a damaging accident
 b. not careful, lack of proper caution
 c. highway safety

9a. with regard to
 b. four
 c. a specific number of eyes
 d. eyeglasses, because individuals who wear glasses are sometimes called "four eyes" by people who wish to offend them

10a. a man at arms serving a nobleman or king
 b. night
 c. after sundown
 d. the moon and stars are seen through the window

HIGHLIGHTED WORD STORY

you; I; break; I, told; you, great; hole; road; you; would; would; towed

HOMOPHONES

Examples:

- a. tolled
  b. rang, pealed
  c. told
  d. made known, revealed
  e. keep a secret

CHAPTER 3
ANSWER KEY

- a. hare
  b. rabbit
  c. hair
  d. what grows on one's head
  e. receding, because that's what happens when the hairline moves back on someone's head

HOMOPHONES I

1a. waste/waist
 b. squander, throw away
 c. part of the body between the chest and the hips
 d. chubby, because your waist gets bigger when you eat a lot of cake

2a. fare
 b. the cost of a ticket
 c. fair
 d. proper, reasonable
 e. airplane ticket

3a. toe
 b. digit at the end of one's foot
 c. tow
 d. to haul, pull
 e. truck, because it is sometimes used to tow a car or truck
 f. foot

4a. which
 b. which one or ones out of a group
 c. witch
 d. a worker of magic who works to heal the sick
 e. a list of doctors' names (a group from which to choose)

5a. tail
 b. a type of seafood
 c. tale
 d. a story, a narration
 e. Once upon a time

6a. scent
 b. an aroma, an odor
 c. cent
 d. a penny, a coin
 e. bill
 f. a beak
 g. paper money
 h. richer, because it seems to refer to an amount of money

CHAPTER 3
ANSWER KEY

7a. son's raise

b. son's increase in salary

c. sun's rays

d. warmth of the sun

e. the woman is basking in the sun

8a. reel

b. part of a fishing rod that pulls in the fishing line

c. real

d. genuine, not an illusion

e. bite and hook, because they both refer to fishing

9a. duel

b. sword fight

c. dual

d. double, having two parts

e. sword fights

10a. waist

b. a part of the body between the chest and hips

c. waste

d. squander, throw away

e. two for one, because it is not wasteful when you pay a low price

HOMOPHONES II

1a. tacks

b. small, flatheaded nails

c. tax

d. charge imposed by authorities on persons or property for public purposes, like income tax

e. collector, which refers to a person to whom people pay their taxes

2a. fowl

b. domestic bird, such as a chicken

c. foul

d. offensive, bad

e. wash your beak out with soap, a practice used by some parents when their children use offensive language

3a. brake

b. use a pedal for slowing or stopping the motion of a vehicle

c. break

d. to treat in a fair, desirable manner (by driving cautiously)

e. repair crew, which refers to a group of people working

CHAPTER 3
ANSWER KEY

4a. "nos"
 b. telling people that they cannot do, see, or say certain things
 c. nose
 d. a part of the face
 e. censors

5a. bawl
 b. crying
 c. ball
 d. a large room for dances
 e. new dad

6a. knead
 b. to press on dough with the hands
 c. need
 d. to require, to want
 e. foolish, because it implies that bakers do something senseless (like selling what they need)

7a. pane
 b. a section, or piece of glass
 c. pain
 d. an unpleasant bodily sensation
 e. glassblower

8a. chew
 b. to crush, grind, or gnaw on with the teeth
 c. choo
 d. a sound a child associates with a train
 e. gum, train

9a. hoarse
 b. having difficulty speaking
 c. horse
 d. an animal that can be ridden
 e. colt, couldn't talk

10a. scenter
 b. used for detecting aromas, odors
 c. center
 d. the middle
 e. middle of your face

HOMOPHONES III

1a. writes
 b. putting words on paper
 c. rites
 d. a ceremonial act performed when someone dies
 e. obituary, because it refers to death

Saying One Thing, Meaning Another

CHAPTER 3
ANSWER KEY

2a. scents
 b. aromas, odors
 c. cents
 d. coins, change, money
 e. money

3a. pear
 b. a type of fruit
 c. pair
 d. two of a kind
 e. twos

4. to put letters on paper; correctly; a last name (Orville Wright)

5. coins, money; detect, perceive; odors, aromas

6. a number; gained a victory in a contest

7. part of the face that bears the nostrils; is aware of, has understanding

8. a number; to have taken in food through one's mouth

9a. tiers
 b. rows (of seats)
 c. tears
 d. crying (with joy)
 e. baseball stadium

10a. dye
 b. to impart a new and often permanent color to fabric
 c. die
 d. to pass from existence, to expire
 e. sew and press, because they also are activities done with fabric

4 DUAL-MEANING SENTENCES

"I once shot an elephant in my pajamas. How he got in my pajamas I'll never know."

Groucho Marx

CHAPTER GOAL

To improve an individual's understanding and use of dual-meaning sentences

TYPES OF AMBIGUITY

This chapter includes activities for two types of sentences that can be taken in two ways.

AMBIGUITY CAUSED BY LINGUISTIC MANIPULATION

Example: He ran his hand through his hair and pulled out a cigar.

AMBIGUITY CAUSED BY SPEAKERS' INTENTIONS

- Indirect Requests
  Example: "That piano playing is giving me a headache."
  (Stop playing the piano.)

- Polite Requests
  Example: "Would you mind helping me with this package?"
  (Help me with this package.)

- Polite Evasions
  Example: "How do you like my new dress?" "It certainly is colorful."

- Ironic Comments
  Example: "You are so lucky." "Yes, the harder I work, the luckier I get."

- Sarcastic Comments
  Example: "Did you just go through a wind tunnel, or is that the latest hairstyle?"

TYPES OF ACTIVITIES PROVIDED

The activities in this chapter allow individuals to analyze dual-meaning sentences in story paragraphs, jokes, riddles, signs, advertisements, cartoons, and comic strips in the following ways:

- determining two meanings and (when possible) rewording to eliminate the ambiguity;

- determining the meaning that might be intended by the speaker for indirect and polite requests, polite evasions, and ironic and sarcastic comments; and

- finding ways to eliminate sarcasm by rewording such utterances.

BACKGROUND INFORMATION

- In sentences that can have two meanings, more than one set relationship can exist among the words and phrases. Finding alternate interpretations requires determining what the words appear to be saying and realizing which words can be implied to change the meaning.

- Finding alternate meanings for ambiguous sentences also may require manipulating and rephrasing sentence segments. For example, consider this ambiguous sentence: "I saw a man eating fish at the beach." One interpretation is simply that a man was having fish for his dinner. The other interpretation uses *man eating* as an adjective descriptor. To clarify the alternate meaning in oral language ("I saw a fish that eats men") would require reordering the words in the sentence, adding the word *that*, changing from singular to plural (man to men), and changing tenses (eating to eats). (Note: In written language, *man eating* would become hyphenated [*man-eating*] to signify an adjective descriptor.)

- In some dual-meaning sentences, the ambiguity occurs primarily because of the speaker's intentions rather than linguistic manipulation. These utterances relay messages according to the goals of the speaker and his or her intended effect of the message on the listener (Lahey, 1988). As previously stated, these types of ambiguous sentences are as follows:

  1. An *indirect request:* "It's very chilly in here. If the window was closed, it would probably get warmer" really means "Someone close the window."

  2. A *polite request:* "Would you mind passing the salt?" really means "Pass the salt."

  3. A *polite evasion,* which is used when someone asks us a question we would rather not answer because to do so would hurt their feelings. Rather than give the hurtful answer, we give another response that the questioner may find acceptable. For example, when replying to the question "Do you think I'm getting too fat?," an individual may respond, "You look very pretty with a full face" instead of "Yes, you are getting too fat."

4. *Ironic and sarcastic utterances,* which are linked because irony becomes sarcasm when the intention is to be hurtful or negative. Both irony and sarcasm are based on stating other than the intended meaning. An ironic comment such as "The harder I work, the luckier I get" really means "It is hard work, not luck, that got me where I am." The individual who uses a sarcastic utterance such as "You'd better not scratch your head, you may get a splinter" really means "You're so stupid, your head must be made out of wood." Sarcastic comments can be cutting, hostile, or contemptuous. They certainly can be hurtful to the recipient of the remark.

DUAL-MEANING SENTENCES

DIRECTIONS

Each item in the dual-meaning sentences activities can have two different meanings. For one of the meanings, you will have to find the words that are implied in the sentence but not used. *Implied* means that the thought is expressed indirectly—that is, the meaning is suggested, rather than stated. If the item is a cartoon or comic strip, examine the pictures closely for clues. Remember, clues can be found in any part of the item. Complete the examples on this page with someone. Then answer the same types of questions on the activity pages that follow.

- He ran his hand through his hair and pulled out a cigar.

    a. What does this sentence appear to be saying? _____

    b. What else could it mean? _____

    c. Reword the comment so that the real meaning is clear. _____

- Look at the cartoon below.

a. What does the sign on the door appear to be saying? _____

b. What does it really mean? _____

c. Which words in the cartoon give you the best clue to the real meaning? _____

d. Reword the sign on the door so that the real meaning is clear. _____

Saying One Thing, Meaning Another

DUAL-MEANING SENTENCES 1

1. Q. Do you think I should get a puppy for my sister?
   A. It sounds like a fair trade to me.

   a. What does the question really mean? _____

   b. How is it interpreted in the answer? _____

   c. Reword the question so that the answer makes sense. _____

2. Mort: "The police are looking for a man with one leg named Smith."
   Don: "What's his other leg called?"

   a. What did Mort mean? _____

   b. What did Don take it to mean? _____

   c. Reword Mort's comment so that his meaning is clear. _____

3. Eric: "Daddy, will you put my shoes on?"
   Daddy: "I'll try, but I don't think they'll fit me."

   a. What did Eric mean? _____

   b. How did Daddy interpret it? _____

   c. Reword Eric's question so that his meaning is clear. _____

4. Cloe: "Will you join me in a bag of peanuts?"
   Joey: "No thanks. I don't think we'll both fit."

   a. What did Cloe mean? _____

   b. How did Joey interpret it? _____

   c. Reword Cloe's question so that her meaning is clear. _____

DUAL-MEANING SENTENCES I

DEWEY: "I CAN LIFT AN ELEPHANT WITH ONE HAND."
HUEY: "I FIND THAT HARD TO BELIEVE."
DEWEY: "SURE I CAN. GET ME AN ELEPHANT WITH ONE HAND AND I'LL SHOW YOU."

5. Look at the cartoon.

   a. What did Dewey mean? _____

   b. What did Huey think he meant? _____

   c. Reword Dewey's first comment so that his meaning is clear. _____

6. Newspaper headline:

   FARMER BILL DIES IN HOUSE

   a. What does this headline really mean? _____

   b. What does it appear to be saying? _____

   c. Reword the headline so that the real meaning is clear. _____

7. Teacher: "Tim, why are you always late for school?"
   Tim: "I'm just obeying the sign near the school."
   Teacher: "What sign is that?"
   Tim: "The sign that says, 'School, Go Slow.'"

   a. What does the sign really mean? _____

   b. How did Tim interpret it? _____

   c. Reword the sign so that the real meaning is clear. _____

Saying One Thing, Meaning Another © 1997 CC Spector. Published by Super Duper® Publications. Duplication permitted for educational use only.

DUAL-MEANING SENTENCES I

8. Look at the cartoon

   a. What does this advertisement really mean?
   _____
   _____

   b. What does it appear to say? _____
   _____
   _____

   c. Reword the advertisement so that the real meaning is clear. _____
   _____
   _____
   _____
   _____
   _____

FOR SALE:
HAVE SEVERAL VERY OLD DRESSES FROM GRANDMOTHER IN BEAUTIFUL CONDITION.

9. Newspaper headline:

   MINERS REFUSE TO WORK AFTER DEATH

   a. What does this headline really mean? _____
   _____

   b. What does it appear to be saying? _____
   _____

   c. Reword the headline so that the real meaning is clear. _____
   _____

10. Two cannibal chiefs were talking after dinner. The first chief said, "Your wife makes a wonderful pot roast." "Yes," replied the second chief. "And I'm certainly going to miss her."

    a. What did the first chief seem to mean by his comment? _____
    _____

    b. What did the second chief's comment lead you to believe? _____
    _____

    c. Which word in this joke gives you a clue to the second chief's response?

DUAL-MEANING SENTENCES I

> PLEASE DO NOT FEED THE ANIMALS. IF YOU HAVE ANY SUITABLE FOOD, GIVE IT TO THE GUARD ON DUTY.

11. Sign in a Budapest zoo:

    a. What does the sign really mean? _____

    _____

    _____

    b. What does it appear to be saying? _____

    _____

    _____

    c. Reword the sign so that the real meaning is clear.

    _____

    _____

    _____

12. Seen in a newspaper: "Yesterday at the beach, Mary Smith was bitten by a spider in a bathing suit."

    a. What does this quote from a newspaper really mean? _____

    _____

    b. What does it appear to be saying? _____

    _____

    c. Reword the quote so that the real meaning is clear. _____

    _____

    _____

DUAL-MEANING SENTENCES II

1. Sign in a dry-cleaning shop:

   Drop your pants here for best results.

   a. What does the sign really mean? _____

   b. What does it appear to be saying? _____

   c. Which words in this item give you a clue about the real meaning? _____

   d. Reword the sign so that the real meaning is clear. _____

2. Newspaper headline:

   SCIENTISTS TO HAVE THE PRESIDENT'S EAR

   a. What does this headline really mean? _____

   b. What does it appear to be saying? _____

   c. Reword the headline so that the real meaning is clear. _____

3. Sign in a Russian cemetery:

   You are welcome to visit this cemetery where famous composers, artists, and writers are buried daily, except Thursday.

   a. What does the sign really mean? _____

   b. What does it appear to be saying? _____

   c. Reword the sign so that the real meaning is clear. _____

DUAL-MEANING SENTENCES II

4. Newspaper headline:

   IRAQI HEAD SEEKS ARMS

   a. What does this headline really mean? _____
   _____

   b. What does it appear to be saying? _____
   _____

   c. Reword the headline so that the real meaning is clear. _____
   _____

5. Look at the cartoon.

ROBIN: "DO YOU REALIZE IT TAKES THREE SHEEP TO MAKE ONE SWEATER?"
TANA: "I DIDN'T EVEN KNOW THAT SHEEP COULD KNIT."

   a. What did Robin mean? _____
   _____

   b. How did Tana interpret it? _____
   _____

   c. Reword Robin's question so that her meaning is clear. _____
   _____

DUAL-MEANING SENTENCES II

6. Newspaper headline:

   NEW AUTOS TO HIT FIVE MILLION

   a. What does this headline really mean? _____
   _____

   b. What does it appear to be saying? _____
   _____

   c. Reword the headline so that the real meaning is clear. _____
   _____

7. Look at the cartoon and the newspaper headline above it.

   a. What does this headline really mean? _____
   _____
   _____

   b. What does it appear to be saying? _____
   _____
   _____

   c. Reword the headline so that the real meaning is clear.
   _____
   _____

8. Did you hear about Manny? He saw a sign in the post office that said "Man wanted for robbery in Pittsburgh." Well, he went in and applied for the job.

   a. What does the sign really mean? _____
   _____

   b. What did Manny think it meant? _____
   _____

   c. Reword the sign so that the real meaning is clear. _____
   _____

DUAL-MEANING SENTENCES II

9. Title of a magazine article:

   KIDS MAKE NUTRITIOUS SNACKS

   a. What does this title really mean? _____
   _____

   b. What does it appear to be saying? _____
   _____

   c. Reword the title so that the real meaning is clear. _____
   _____

10. Look at the cartoon below:

   a. What did Hagar's wife mean? _____

   b. What did Hagar take it to mean? _____

   c. What do you see in the comic strip that gives you clues to what is meant by Hagar's wife and by Hagar? _____
   _____
   _____
   _____

11. Mother: "Lucy, aren't you going to the party?"
    Lucy: "No, mother. The invitation said three to six, and I'm seven."

   a. Which part of Lucy's comment can be taken in two ways? _____
   _____

   b. What does it really mean? _____

   c. What did Lucy take it to mean? _____

   d. Which word can be added to the invitation to make the meaning clear?
   _____

DUAL-MEANING SENTENCES II

12. Look at the cartoon:

LAST WEEK AT THE BEACH, I SAW A MAN EATING FISH.

a. What does this comment mean in the first part of this cartoon? _____

b. What does it mean in the second part of this cartoon? _____

c. Reword the comment so that the meaning of the first part of the cartoon is made clear. _____

d. Reword the comment so that the meaning of the second part of the cartoon is made clear. _____

DUAL-MEANING SENTENCES III

1. Julie: "So, your baby is due in October. Do you want a boy or a girl?"
   Caroline: "Yes."

   a. Which sentence can be taken in two ways? _____

   b. What did Julie mean? _____

   c. What did Caroline mean? _____

2. The doctor was surprised that Mary had a little lamb.

   a. What does this sentence appear to be saying? _____

   b. What else can it mean? _____

   c. Which words give you a clue to what the sentence appears to be saying?
   _____

3. Headline in a golf magazine:

   GRANDMOTHER OF EIGHT MAKES HOLE IN ONE

   a. What does this headline really mean? _____

   b. What does it appear to be saying? _____

   c. Which words in this item give you a clue to the real meaning? _____

   d. Reword the headline so that the real meaning is clear. _____

4. Linda: "I've been skiing since I was six years old."
   Louise: "Wow. You must be very tired."

   a. What did Linda mean? _____

   b. How did Louise interpret it? _____

   c. Reword Linda's comment so that her meaning is clear. _____

Saying One Thing, Meaning Another

DUAL-MEANING SENTENCES III

5. Magazine headline:
   COSMETIC SURGERY FOR WOMEN MUSHROOMS

   a. What does this headline really mean? _____
   _____

   b. What does it appear to be saying? _____
   _____

   c. Reword the headline so that the real meaning is clear. _____
   _____

6. Joe: "Why are you so lazy? Don't you know that exercise kills germs?"
   Moe: "Great. Now all we have to do is figure out how to get germs to exercise."

   a. What does Joe mean? _____

   b. What did Moe take it to mean? _____

   c. Reword Joe's comment so that his meaning is clear. _____
   _____

7. Newspaper headline:
   STOLEN PAINTING FOUND BY TREE

   a. What does this headline really mean? _____
   _____

   b. What does it appear to be saying? _____
   _____

   c. Reword the headline so that the real meaning is clear. _____
   _____

8. Newspaper headline:
   RED TAPE HOLDS UP NEW BRIDGE

   a. What does this headline really mean? _____
   _____

   b. What does it appear to be saying? _____
   _____

   c. Reword the headline so that the real meaning is clear. _____
   _____

Chapter 4

DUAL-MEANING SENTENCES III

9. Rita: "You can't park your car here."
   Lolita: "Why not? The sign says 'Fine for parking.'"

   a. What does the sign really mean? _____

   b. What did Lolita take it to mean? _____

   c. Reword the sign so that the real meaning is clear. _____
   _____

10. Newspaper headline:

    LOCAL HIGH SCHOOL DROPOUTS CUT IN HALF

    a. What does this headline really mean? _____
    _____

    b. What does it appear to be saying? _____
    _____

    c. Reword the headline so that the real meaning is clear. _____
    _____

11. Newspaper headline:

    HOSPITALS SUED BY SEVEN FOOT DOCTORS

    a. What does this headline really mean? _____
    _____

    b. What does it appear to be saying? _____
    _____

    c. Reword the headline so that the real meaning is clear. _____
    _____

12. Newspaper headline:

    DRUNK GETS NINE MONTHS IN VIOLIN CASE

    a. What does this headline really mean? _____
    _____

    b. What does it appear to be saying? _____
    _____

    c. Reword the headline so that the real meaning is clear. _____
    _____

DUAL-MEANING SENTENCES: INDIRECT AND POLITE REQUESTS

DID YOU KNOW...

The ambiguity in the following items are caused by the speaker's intentions. The meaning has to be figured out from what we know about the speaker and the situation. In our everyday conversations, we frequently make and respond to indirect and polite requests. We use our inferencing skills to figure out what is really being requested. For example, "Do you know the way to Main Street?" is an indirect way of saying "Tell me how to get to Main Street." Likewise, "Is your mother at home?" is a polite way of saying "Let me speak to your mother." The salesperson who is asked, "Do these shorts come in size 8?" understands that the customer is saying, "I want these shorts in size 8."

DIRECTIONS

Each of the following items contains an indirect or polite request that can be figured out from the context of the paragraph. Use your inferencing skills to determine what the speaker is really requesting. Complete the example below with someone, then do the items that follow.

- "You really seem to be enjoying your new stereo. Wouldn't it sound better if the music was softer? Loud music always gives me a headache."

   What message is the speaker trying to convey?_____

   _____

1. "Gosh, that's a really big piece of chocolate cake you're eating. It looks delicious. I hardly ever get a chance to eat really good chocolate cake."

   What message is the speaker trying to convey?_____

   _____

2. "You know, Grandma, all of my friends are getting new dresses for the prom. Mom says we can't afford a dress right now because we have to pay for the new car. I guess I'll have to look like a dork in my old blue dress. Maybe I won't even go!"

   What message is the speaker trying to convey?_____

   _____

DUAL-MEANING SENTENCES: INDIRECT AND POLITE REQUESTS

3. "I love your new kitchen curtains. I wish I could sew the way you do; then I'd make some for my kitchen. You say it only took you an hour to make them? At Clara's curtain shop, I will probably have to pay five times the amount you paid for fabric."

   What message is the speaker trying to convey? _____
   _____

4. "It's such a hot day. I would love to go to the beach. If only my car wasn't in the repair shop. You're lucky you don't have any problems with your car."

   What message is the speaker trying to convey? _____
   _____

5. "Those muffins sure smell good. All I had for breakfast this morning was orange juice and a vitamin. I didn't realize I'd be so hungry."

   What message is the speaker trying to convey? _____
   _____

6. "It's so warm in here. It would be more comfortable if the windows were opened."

   What is the speaker requesting? _____
   _____

7. "Is it cold in here, or is it just me?"

   What message is the speaker trying to convey? _____
   _____

8. "Is the children's zoo in this direction?"

   What is the speaker requesting? _____
   _____

9. "You know, Dad, if I had a bigger allowance I could sharpen my money-management skills."

   What message is the speaker trying to convey? _____
   _____

10. "Do you think that cute blonde has a boyfriend?"

    What message is the speaker trying to convey? _____
    _____

Saying One Thing, Meaning Another

DUAL-MEANING SENTENCES: INDIRECT AND POLITE REQUESTS

11. Waiter in a restaurant: "How was your dessert, sir? Can I get you anything else?"

    What message is the speaker trying to convey?_____

    _____

12. "It's too bad I put on my expensive new shoes. Those puddles from last night's rain are going to make it hard for me to get to the mailbox."

    What message is the speaker trying to convey?_____

    _____

DUAL-MEANING SENTENCES: POLITE EVASIONS

DID YOU KNOW...

At times we are asked questions that are difficult to answer without hurting the questioner's feelings. Remaining silent would be awkward, so rather than giving a direct answer to the question, we respond with polite evasions.

DIRECTIONS

Each of the following items contain polite evasions that are open to interpretation by the listener. Use your inferencing skills to find a probable cause for each of the following polite evasions. Complete the example below with someone, then do the items that follow.

- "What do you think of my new outfit?"
  "Well, it certainly is colorful."

  What might the responder be trying to avoid saying? _____
  _____

1. "How do you like my haircut?"
   "It certainly is short."

   What might the responder be trying to avoid saying? _____
   _____

2. "What did you think of my brother's singing at the recital last night?"
   "He has a powerful voice."

   What might the responder be trying to avoid saying? _____
   _____

3. "Would you care for some more of the stew?"
   "No, thank you, I'm saving room for dessert."

   What might the responder be trying to avoid saying? _____
   _____

4. "I can lend you this dress if you would rather not go out in jeans."
   "No, that's okay. I'll manage."

   What might the responder be trying to avoid saying? _____
   _____

5. "Would you care to dance?"
   "Thank you, but I'm waiting for my friend."

   What might the responder be trying to avoid saying? _____
   _____

DUAL-MEANING SENTENCES: POLITE EVASIONS

6. "Do you think my dress is too short?"

   "Well, many different lengths are fashionable these days."

   What might the responder be trying to avoid saying? _____
   _____

7. "Will you be coming to the party tomorrow?"

   "I'll have to think about it."

   What might the responder be trying to avoid saying? _____
   _____

8. "Can we get together for dinner sometime?"

   "I hardly ever have time to go out for dinner."

   What might the responder be trying to avoid saying? _____
   _____

9. "Care to see a movie tonight?"

   "Sorry, I have to visit my grandmother."

   What might the responder be trying to avoid saying? _____
   _____

10. "This is my new baby sister. Isn't she adorable?"

    "Wow, look at all that hair!"

    What might the responder be trying to avoid saying? _____
    _____

11. "Don't you think Patricia is just the most beautiful girl in her sorority?"

    "Well, she certainly fits in with that lovely group."

    What might the responder be trying to avoid saying? _____
    _____

12. "I'm looking for a new job. Would you mind writing a letter of recommendation for me?"

    "I'm not very good at writing that kind of letter."

    What might the responder be trying to avoid saying? _____
    _____

DUAL-MEANING SENTENCES: IRONIC UTTERANCES

DID YOU KNOW...

Ironic comments are utterances that state one meaning when, often, the opposite meaning is intended. Irony frequently is used to comment on the annoyances we encounter in our everyday lives. For example, we might say, "Don't you just love waiting for traffic lights to turn green?" when we really mean we are annoyed about having to wait. At times, ironic utterances are attempts to be humorous. For example, a woman falls and breaks her leg. Her friend accidentally causes her pain by trying to remove her shoes so she would be more comfortable while waiting for an ambulance. The friend says, "There, isn't that a lot better?" when she really means, "I'm sorry I hurt you while trying to help you." Irony can become sarcasm if the speaker's intention is to be nasty, cutting, or contemptuous.

DIRECTIONS

Use your inferencing skills to figure out the intended meaning of the ironic comments in the following items. Be sure to consider what is known about the situation and the speaker. Complete the example below with someone, then do the items that follow.

- Randy to Mandy, who just got a big promotion at work:
  "You are so lucky."
  Mandy: "Yes, the harder I work, the luckier I get."

  What is Mandy really saying? _____
  _____

1. Liz comes home with an A on a math exam. Her mother had told her she had the ability to do well all along, but Liz didn't believe her. Her mother looks at the A and says, "I guess you really aren't very good at math after all."

   a. What is Liz's mother really saying? _____
   _____

   b. How could her mother say what she means without being ironic?
   _____

2. Peter is standing in line waiting for a theater to open. He says, "Time sure flies when you're having fun."

   a. What does Peter really mean? _____

   b. How could Peter say what he means without being ironic?
   _____

Saying One Thing, Meaning Another

DUAL-MEANING SENTENCES: IRONIC UTTERANCES

3. Gwen to a coworker: "I just love getting up early to go to work every Monday morning. It sure beats sleeping late on the weekends."

    a. What does Gwen really mean? _____
    _____

    b. How could Gwen say what she means without being ironic?
    _____

4. Message on a poster: "Lost Dog: Reward to Finder! Front right paw missing, part of one ear is ripped off, and he can't see out of his left eye. Answers to the name of Lucky."

    a. What is ironic about this poster? _____
    _____

    b. Could the poster be changed so that it is not ironic? _____
    _____

5. "Help stamp out, eliminate, and abolish redundancy."

    a. What is ironic about this comment? _____
    _____

    b. How could this statement be changed so that it is not ironic?
    _____

6. "A good deed seldom goes unpunished."

    a. What is ironic about this comment? _____
    _____

    b. How can the same thought be expressed without being ironic?
    _____

7. Ninety-seven-year-old man to his grandson: "It's wonderful that I've won the lottery. Now I have enough money to take a leisurely trip around the world."

    a. What is ironic about this comment? _____
    _____

    b. How could the 97-year-old man say what he means without being ironic? _____

DUAL-MEANING SENTENCES: IRONIC UTTERANCES

8. Doris: "Anytime I want to be sure I'll meet some friends, I just go to the supermarket looking wretched."

   a. What is ironic about this comment? _____

   _____

   b. How could Doris say what she means without being ironic? _____

   _____

9. Fran to Frank: "If I prepare enough food for 20 people, 40 will come to the party. If I prepare enough food for 40 people, 20 will come."

   a. What is ironic about this comment? _____

   _____

   b. How could Fran say what she means without being ironic? _____

   _____

10. Priscilla to a coworker: "The more I hurry, the farther behind I seem to get."

    a. What is ironic about this comment? _____

    _____

    b. How could Priscilla say what she means without being ironic? _____

    _____

11. Lorraine to Jimmy: "I'm going to water the garden this morning. Then we can be sure it's going to rain this afternoon."

    a. What is ironic about this comment? _____

    _____

    b. How could Lorraine say what she means without being ironic? _____

    _____

12. Dorothy to Harry: "I always seem to dress too casually for Mary Lou's parties. This time I wore my best dress and it turns out to be a pool party."

    a. What is ironic about this comment? _____

    _____

    b. How could Dorothy say what she means without being ironic? _____

    _____

DUAL-MEANING SENTENCES: SARCASTIC UTTERANCES

DID YOU KNOW...

Sarcastic comments, like ironic comments, state one meaning when the opposite meaning is intended. However, unlike ironic comments, sarcastic comments are intended to be nasty, cutting, or contemptuous. At times, we hear people using sarcastic remarks because they think they are witty. They forget that wit is meant to amuse, not abuse. At times, sarcasm is not easy to detect from the words that are said. Often the speaker's tone of voice indicates that the intention is to be nasty or contemptuous. It is not possible to eliminate sarcasm in jokes, because that is the basis of the humor. Sarcastic remarks in jokes are not hurtful unless they are directed at real people.

DIRECTIONS

Use your inferencing skills to figure out the intended meaning of each comment. Because we are reading the sarcastic comments in the items below, we cannot make use of the speaker's tone of voice to give us a clue. Instead, our understanding will depend on knowing something about the situation and the speaker who makes the comment. Tell how to eliminate the sarcasm by making the comment in a different way. Complete the example below with someone, then do the items that follow.

- Mike comes home with his clothing extremely dirty after playing football. His sister, Mary, is in a bad mood because she had to stay in and clean her room. She looks at him and says, "Well, if you aren't the picture of cleanliness."

    What is Mary really saying to her brother Mike? _____

    _____

    How could she say what she means without being sarcastic? _____

    _____

    _____

1. A woman is trying to get her husband to lose weight. She plans healthy meals and encourages him to exercise. Her husband does not make an effort to either diet or exercise. At the dinner table, she says, "Would you like a small piece of this cake, or should I just give you the whole thing?"

    a. What is the woman really telling her husband? _____

    _____

    b. How could she say what she means without being sarcastic? _____

    _____

    _____

DUAL-MEANING SENTENCES: SARCASTIC UTTERANCES

2. Lisa: "Whenever I'm down in the dumps, I buy myself a new hat."
   Janey: "Oh, so that's where you get them."

   a. What does Lisa mean by "down in the dumps"? _____
   _____

   b. How could Janey say what she means without being sarcastic?
   _____

3. Jimmy repeatedly misses the hoop in a basketball game. His friend Paul says, "Boy, you really are a terrific shot."

   a. What is Paul really saying to Jimmy? _____
   _____

   b. How could Paul say what he means without being sarcastic?
   _____

4. Nasty teacher to a student who has difficulty figuring out a math problem: "Watch out when you scratch your head. You may get a splinter."

   a. What is the teacher really saying to the student? _____
   _____

   b. How could the teacher say what she means without being sarcastic?
   _____
   _____

5. Danny is trying to get away from John because he is always talking about himself.
   John: "I throw myself into everything I undertake."
   Danny: "Perhaps you should go and dig a deep well."

   a. What is Danny really saying to John? _____
   _____

   b. How could Danny say what he means without being sarcastic?
   _____

DUAL-MEANING SENTENCES: SARCASTIC UTTERANCES

6. Marie's glasses fell off, and she is about to pick them up when Nicky steps on them.

    Marie: "Watch out! Oh no! You've broken my glasses. Isn't that just great. I'm so glad you came here today."

    a. What did Marie really mean? _____
    _____

    b. How could Marie say what she means without being sarcastic?
    _____

7. A teacher is annoyed with a student who always calls out in class but generally does not have the correct answers. He says to the student, "Oh yes, we all know how clever you are."

    a. What does the teacher really mean? _____
    _____

    b. How could the teacher say what he means without being sarcastic?
    _____

8. Tim is annoyed with his big brother, who always insists he is right when they discuss sports trivia. He says to his brother, "Well, Mr. Know-it-all, what's the answer this time?"

    a. What did Tim really mean?_____
    _____

    b. How could Tim say what he means without being sarcastic?
    _____

9. Mary is discussing a boy she dislikes: "Offer him a penny for his thoughts, and you're being more than generous."

    a. What is Mary really saying about the boy?_____
    _____

    b. What could Mary say about the boy without being sarcastic?
    _____

DUAL-MEANING SENTENCES: SARCASTIC UTTERANCES

10. Josie to a man who is pestering her for a date: "You are my idea of the perfect date—not!"

    a. What does Josie really mean? _____
    _____

    b. How could Josie say what she means without being sarcastic?
    _____

11. Lulu's indecisiveness annoys her friend Belle.
    Lulu: "I've changed my mind."
    Belle: "Does the new one work any better?"

    a. What does Belle really mean? _____
    _____

    b. How could Belle say what she means without being sarcastic?
    _____

12. Yoshi to a friend whose hair is messy: "Did you just go through a wind tunnel, or is that the latest hair style?"

    a. What is Yoshi really saying? _____
    _____

    b. How could Yoshi say what he means without being sarcastic?
    _____

ADDITIONAL ACTIVITIES

1. Encourage individuals to examine newspapers, magazines, cartoons, and comic strips for examples of dual-meaning sentences. Collect these examples in a book, and use them as a basis for ongoing discussions.

2. Have individuals collect from various settings (e.g., at home, at school, on television, in movies, in conversations with peers, etc.) comments that are ambiguous because of speakers' intentions. Discuss what the intended meanings of such comments might be.

3. Have individuals read (or say) ironic or sarcastic comments aloud in an ironic or sarcastic manner. Discuss what makes the comments sound ironic or sarcastic (e.g., tone of voice, facial expression, stress or intonation pattern, gestures, etc.).

CHAPTER 4 ANSWER KEY

These answers are merely guidelines. The facilitator can judge if the individual's responses are appropriate for each item.

DUAL-MEANING SENTENCES

Examples:

- a. He pulled a cigar out of his hair.

  b. After he ran his hand through his hair, he pulled a cigar out of his pocket.

  c. He ran his hand through his hair, and then he pulled a cigar out of his pocket. (Explain that by adding the implied words *and then* and *out of his pocket,* we state what the comment really means.)

- a. Please leave and don't come in.

  b. Please let us help you with your travel plans.

  c. Travel Agency (on the sign)

  d. Please let us arrange a trip for you.

DUAL-MEANING SENTENCES I

1a. Should I buy a puppy to give to my sister?

b. trade his sister for a puppy

c. Do you think I should exchange my sister for a puppy?

2a. A man named Smith has one leg.

b. The leg's name is Smith.

c. The police are looking for a man named Smith who has one leg.

3a. Help me put my shoes on my feet.

b. Eric wanted Daddy to wear Eric's shoes.

c. Daddy, will you help me put on my shoes?

4a. share my peanuts, eat them with me

b. get into the bag of peanuts

c. Would you like to share a bag of peanuts with me?

5a. The elephant has one hand.

b. Dewey was strong enough to lift the elephant with one of his hands.

c. I can lift an elephant that has one hand.

6a. A legislative bill affecting farmers does not receive enough support to pass in the House of Representatives.

b. A farmer named Bill dies in a house.

c. Farmer Legislation Dies in House

7a. People in vehicles should drive slowly near the school.

b. Students should walk slowly when approaching the school.

c. School, Vehicles Go Slow

CHAPTER 4
ANSWER KEY

8a. For sale: Grandmother's dresses that are in beautiful condition

b. Grandmother is in beautiful condition.

c. For sale: Several of my grandmother's dresses in beautiful condition.

9a. Miners refuse to work after the death of a fellow miner.

b. Miners refuse to work after they die.

c. Miners Refuse to Work after Coworker's Death

10a. Your wife is a good cook.

b. They had eaten his wife as their meal.

c. cannibal, because they eat human beings

11a. The guard will give the food to the animals.

b. Feed the guard.

c. Please do not feed the animals. If you have any suitable food, give it to the guard on duty and he will feed them.

12a. Mary Smith, who was wearing a bathing suit, was bitten by a spider.

b. The spider was wearing a bathing suit.

c. Yesterday at the beach, Mary Smith, clad in a bathing suit, was bitten by a spider.

DUAL-MEANING SENTENCES II

1a. Leave your pants here to be cleaned.

b. Let your pants fall down in this shop.

c. dry-cleaning shop

d. For best results, have your pants cleaned here.

2a. The president will listen to what a group of scientists have to say.

b. The president's ear will be taken from his head and given to the scientists.

c. Scientists to Talk with the President

3a. You can visit the cemetery every day except Thursday.

b. Composers, artists, and writers are being buried there every day except Thursday.

c. You are welcome to visit this cemetery where famous composers, artists, and writers are buried. Open every day except Thursday.

4a. The head (leader) of the Iraqi government is looking for weapons.

b. A head from Iraq is looking for arms (parts of the body).

c. Iraqi Leader Seeks Weapons

5a. The wool from three sheep goes into one sweater.

b. The sheep do the knitting.

c. Do you realize it takes the wool from three sheep to make one sweater?

6a. Five million new cars will be built.

b. New cars will hit five million people.

c. Five Million New Cars to Be Built

CHAPTER 4
ANSWER KEY

7a. Police help a victim who has been bitten by a dog.
   b. The police are helping the dog bite the victim.
   c. Dog-bite Victim Helped by Police

8a. Someone was looking for the man (a robber) to arrest him.
   b. They were looking for someone to commit a robbery.
   c. Pittsburgh Police Seek Man Who Committed Robbery

9a. Kids prepare nutritious snacks.
   b. If you want a nutritious snack, eat kids.
   c. Kids Prepare Nutritious Snacks

10a. Do you want coffee?
    b. Is this coffee?
    c. Hagar's wife is standing near him ready to pour coffee from the pot, and Hagar looks in the coffee pot to see what is in it.

11a. The invitation said three to six.
    b. three to six o'clock
    c. three to six years of age
    d. o'clock

12a. A man at the beach was eating fish.
    b. A fish that is a man-eater was seen at the beach.
    c. Last week at the beach, I saw a man who was eating fish.
    d. Last week at the beach, I saw a fish that was a man-eater.

DUAL-MEANING SENTENCES III

1a. Do you want a boy or a girl?
   b. Which gender would you prefer?
   c. I don't care whether it is a boy or a girl, I want either one.

2a. Mary gave birth to a little lamb.
   b. Mary had a little lamb as a pet, or Mary ate a small portion of lamb for her dinner.
   c. doctor was surprised

3a. A grandmother, who has eight grandchildren, makes a hole in one while playing golf.
   b. A grandmother makes a hole in one of her eight grandchildren.
   c. golf magazine
   d. Hole in One Hit by Grandmother of Eight

CHAPTER 4 ANSWER KEY

4a. I've known how to ski since I was six years old.

b. Linda has been skiing for years without stopping.

c. I learned how to ski when I was six years old.

5a. There is tremendous growth in the number of women who are having cosmetic surgery.

b. Female mushrooms are having cosmetic surgery.

c. Number of Women Having Cosmetic Surgery Mushrooms

6a. If you exercise, the germs will die.

b. If the germs exercise, they will die.

c. Don't you know that when you exercise it kills germs?

7a. The stolen painting was found near a tree.

b. The tree found a stolen painting.

c. Stolen Painting Found Near Tree

8a. Unnecessary bureaucratic routines delay the building of a new bridge.

b. Tape that is red is supporting the new bridge.

c. Bureaucracy Delays Progress on New Bridge

9a. You must pay money (a penalty) for parking in this spot, because you're not supposed to park here.

b. It's a good place to park.

c. Penalty for Parking Here

10a. Half as many local high school students are dropping out.

b. The students who drop out of high school are cut in half.

c. Half as Many Local High School Students Drop Out

11a. Seven doctors who specialize in foot problems are suing hospitals.

b. Doctors who are seven feet tall are suing hospitals.

c. Hospitals Sued by Seven Podiatrists

12a. A drunk has to go to prison for nine months in a legal case that involves a violin.

b. A drunk will have to spend nine months in a case made to hold a violin.

c. Drunk Gets Nine Months in Case Involving Violin

DUAL-MEANING SENTENCES: INDIRECT AND POLITE REQUESTS

Example:

- Turn down the stereo.

1. I would like to have some of your chocolate cake.

2. Grandma, can you buy me a prom dress?

3. Would you make kitchen curtains for me? It wouldn't take you long.

CHAPTER 4
ANSWER KEY

4. Please take me to the beach.

5. I would like to have a muffin.

6. Please open the windows.

7. Turn up the heat.

8. Tell me how to get to the children's zoo.

9. I would like a bigger allowance.

10. I'm interested in that cute blonde. Find out if she's available.

11. If you're finished eating, please leave so others can use this table.

12. Please go out and get the mail for me.

DUAL-MEANING SENTENCES: POLITE EVASIONS

Example:

- "I don't really like your new outfit."

    Being colorful can be viewed as a positive comment even though it was not an answer to the question that was asked. This ambiguous response allows the questioner to interpret the response in a manner that is least hurtful.

1. I don't really like the haircut.

2. He's loud, but he doesn't have a good voice.

3. The stew isn't good enough to want another helping.

4. Although the jeans are not ideal, they are better than the dress that was offered.

5. I'd rather not dance with you.

6. Yes, your dress is too short.

7. Probably not.

8. No, I'd rather not.

9. No, I wouldn't care to see a movie with you.

10. She has lots of hair, but she's not that adorable.

11. She's pretty, but she's not the most beautiful girl in the sorority.

12. I'd rather not write a letter of recommendation for you.

CHAPTER 4 ANSWER KEY

DUAL-MEANING SENTENCES: IRONIC UTTERANCES

Example:

- The reason I got promoted was because I work hard, not because I'm lucky. Randy may have been saying it was luck to explain why she didn't get a promotion too.

1a. See, I told you that you are a good math student.
 b. "I see all your studying paid off."

2a. He's hoping the theater will be opened soon because he's tired of waiting.
 b. "It's annoying to stand and wait so long."

3a. She really does not like to get up early on Monday mornings.
 b. "I hate getting up early to go to work every Monday. I prefer weekends because I can sleep late."

4a. The dog's name is Lucky and he seems to have been very unlucky during his life.
 b. Yes, if the dog had a name other than Lucky, or if the poster listed a phone number instead of the dog's name.

5a. The comment itself is very redundant.
 b. "Help eliminate redundancy."

6a. We expect a good deed to be rewarded and a bad deed to be punished.
 b. We don't usually get what we deserve.

7a. The man won the lottery at age 97. He probably is too old to take a leisurely trip around the world.
 b. "It's too bad I didn't win the lottery when I was young enough to use the money to take a leisurely trip around the world."

8a. We usually don't want to meet anyone we know when we don't look well.
 b. "I don't want to go to the supermarket when I look wretched, because I am likely to meet someone I know."

9a. Whatever we prepare for, the opposite is likely to happen.
 b. "I don't know how many people will come to the party, so it's difficult to decide how much food to prepare."

10a. When we hurry, we expect to catch up, not fall behind.
 b. "No matter how much I hurry, I can't seem to catch up on my work."

CHAPTER 4 ANSWER KEY

11a. It always seems to rain after we spend the time and effort to water the garden.

b. "The time and effort I will spend watering the garden this morning will be wasted if it rains this afternoon."

12a. The one time when casual clothing would be appropriate, I am all dressed up.

b. "I never seem to wear the right clothing to Mary Lou's parties."

DUAL-MEANING SENTENCES: SARCASTIC UTTERANCES

Example:

- You look very dirty.

   Your clothes really get dirty when you play football. (This is an observation rather than a nasty personal comment.)

1a. You're too fat to be eating cake, so if you want any it should be a small piece, but I know from past experience you'll eat more than you should.

b. "Would you like a small piece of cake?"

2a. Feeling sad

b. "I've noticed your taste in hats is different from mine." (or say nothing)

3a. You're terrible at making baskets (getting the ball through the hoop).

b. "Looks like you missed again." (or say nothing)

4a. You're such a slow thinker, your head must be made of wood.

b. "Looks like you don't know the answer."

5a. Dig a deep well so you can throw yourself in it.

b. "I'd rather not hear so much about your undertakings." (or say nothing)

6a. I'm sorry you are here. If you had not come, my glasses wouldn't have been broken.

b. "I wish you had been more careful."

7a. Based on your past performance, I don't expect much from you.

b. "Don't call out the answers."

8a. You always think you know more than I do.

b. "Well, what is the answer?"

9a. He is not an intelligent person, so his thoughts are worthless.

b. "He's not too smart."

CHAPTER 4
ANSWER KEY

10a. I don't want to go out with you.

   b. "I'd rather not go out with you."

11a. Your mind is not very good because you can't make decisions.

   b. "I wish you wouldn't change your mind so often."

12a. Your hair looks as if it has been blown by a strong wind.

   b. "You need to comb your hair. It's very messy."

5

Telegram sent by Dorothy Parker to a friend who had just had a baby:

"Congratulations! We all knew you had it in you!"

MULTIPLE MEANING PHRASES

CHAPTER GOAL

To improve an individual's understanding and use of multiple meaning phrases

TYPES OF ACTIVITIES PROVIDED

This chapter includes activities for examining multiple meaning phrases presented mainly in the form of idiomatic expressions. (Note: Several of these activities require the use of an idiom or proverb dictionary—see Appendix D.) These activities include:

- using context clues to determine the appropriate meaning of idioms;
- analyzing paragraphs that contain numerous idioms;
- analyzing idioms and proverbs in jokes, riddles, cartoons, comic strips, signs, and advertisements;
- matching idioms and proverbs to their definitions;
- matching idioms and proverbs to their counterparts from other countries;
- comparing idioms that mean the same thing;
- contrasting idioms and proverbs that have opposite meanings;
- defining idioms that have only a figurative meaning;
- matching fixed-order idioms to their definitions; and
- figuring out multiple meaning phrase "drawings."

BACKGROUND INFORMATION

- Some multiple meaning phrases are merely a group of words that can have two meanings. For example, "We are having a *three-day sale*." (Great. I'll take Friday, Saturday, and Sunday.) Other multiple meaning phrases—idioms, metaphors, similes, and proverbs—are forms of figurative language. While all of these forms appear in written materials, it is the idiomatic expression that is prominent in spontaneous conversational language. In fact, idioms are used frequently, proverbs are used occasionally, but similes and metaphors occur rarely in spontaneous conversations or in the language of instruction (Lazar, Warr-Leeper, Beel-Nicholson, and Johnson, 1989). The materials gathered for this book were taken from frequently used everyday language, and therefore, with a few exceptions (such as proverbs), idioms are the form of figurative language examined.

- Not understanding idioms could be devastating, since two-thirds of the English language contains such ambiguities (Boatner and Gates, 1975; Arnold and Hornett, 1990). Practically speaking, it is essential to learn idioms. If we do not use idiomatic expressions in everyday conversations, our speech sounds stilted, unnatural, or childlike. Unless we understand idioms, it is not possible to truly comprehend what we read and hear in many of our conversations.

- Children as young as eight years old can grasp some of the linguistic ambiguity of idioms in the context of humor. Just how easy or difficult it will be to understand idioms will depend, to a great extent, on the inherent nature of each idiom (Spector, 1996).

- Idioms can be transparent or opaque (referring to the degree to which an idiom's meaning can be figured out from the individual words in the idiom). *She's skating on thin ice*, for example, is relatively transparent. The words imply danger and lead to the idiom's meaning. Also somewhat transparent is the expression *my lips are sealed*. If one's lips were sealed together, it would be impossible to talk. It would be necessary to keep quiet about something. However, opaque idioms such as *face the music* (incur the penalty) or *have a soft spot* (be partial to or have affection for someone) are far more difficult because it is not possible to figure out their meanings from the individual words.

- Idioms, in general, are expressions that can have more than one meaning depending on the linguistic context. For example, the expression *down in the dumps* can be interpreted literally as a place where garbage is brought if the context concerns location, or it can be interpreted figuratively as being sad if the context concerns mood. Many idioms are dichotomous, having one literal and one figurative meaning.

- Some idioms have two figurative meanings. *Give someone a hand* could mean to help someone or to applaud. This expression, as an idiom, does not have a literal interpretation in a generally accepted sense. There are even some idioms that can be interpreted only in one figurative sense and not at all literally (for example, *fall in love, on the spur of the moment*, or *throw a party*).

- Some idioms have a multitude of meanings. *Hold up*, for example, can mean to raise or lift ("Hold up your hand if you know the answer"), to support ("I don't think that tiny chair can hold up an adult"), to show or exhibit ("Hold up your model airplane so everyone can see it"), to stop or impede ("The snowstorm will probably hold up traffic"), to rob at gunpoint ("The masked man tried to hold up the bank"), to remain calm or keep control of oneself ("She tried to hold up at the funeral for the sake of her children"), to continue in the same condition without losing effectiveness ("Our team can hold up even under pressure"), and to prove true ("Joe's story did not hold up under close scrutiny").

- At times, using idioms is more effective than simple, straightforward language. Terrell (1996) discussed the impact that using specific idioms can have on individuals in a culturally and linguistically diverse group. She stated that, in a testing situation, verbal praise stated in culturally relevant idioms such as *good job blood* or *right on, brother* led to higher scores for African American students on intelligence tests than comments such as *fine* or *good*.

- Researchers have recognized just how formidable a task idiom comprehension can be (Kamhi, 1987; van Kleeck, 1984). The metalinguistic skills needed for understanding ambiguities are complex. Especially challenging are the skills required for showing comprehension of the ambiguity of idioms. For example, an individual would have to be able to explain multiple meanings for a group of words that mean something other than the sum of the meanings of the individual words.

- Idioms may be learned as giant lexical units, as Ackerman (1982) and Hoffman and Honeck (1980) suggest. This seems probable for opaque idioms. However, for idioms that are relatively transparent, the figurative meaning often can be inferred from the words that comprise the idiom (Nippold and Rudzinski, 1993).

- Although proverbs are not the focus of this chapter, several of them can be found in some of the activities that follow. Proverbs offer a bit of advice on moral or practical behavior. Like idioms, proverbs can be interpreted literally and figuratively (for example, *Don't put all your eggs in one basket*). Studies by Nippold, Martin, and Erskine (1988) and Honeck, Sowry, and Voegtle (1978) showed that although proverbs are thought to be the most difficult type of figurative language, when proverb tasks are presented properly, it is possible even for preadolescents to understand them.

- Using an explanation task, Nippold, Uhden, and Schwarz (1997) found that adolescents and young adults learn proverbs through active analysis of the words they contain.

- Some researchers (Ackerman, 1982; Gibbs, 1986; Nelson, 1987) have expressed concern about presenting the literal version of a word or phrase. It was thought that doing so may cause confusion or be a hindrance when assessing comprehension and may not be necessary for ultimately understanding the idiom's figurative meaning. However, this is not the case with respect to intervention. Given that much of the ambiguous material encountered in everyday life (such as cartoons, comic strips, and advertisements) depicts the literal version of multiple meaning words and phrases, it is important that individuals have numerous opportunities to examine and interpret such material. In fact, it is often the contrast between literal and figurative meanings in cartoons, comic strips, and advertisements that make them humorous.

HIGHLIGHTED IDIOMS

DIRECTIONS

Each of the highlighted (bold-faced) phrases in the following items is an idiom that does not mean exactly what it appears to be saying. Some idioms can be figured out by considering the thought expressed by the words in the phrase. Look at the idiom *my lips are sealed*, for example. What would happen if your lips were sealed together? You would not be able to talk. You would have to keep quiet about something. Sometimes idioms can be figured out by looking at what they are likely to mean in a story. Complete the example items below with someone. Then figure out the meaning of the highlighted idioms in the items on the activity pages that follow.

- Every time I go out for dinner with you, I'm so embarrassed. You order enough food for two people and eat every bit of it. You're going to get very fat if you don't stop **eating like a horse**.

    a. Without the story, what do the words in the highlighted phrase seem to be saying? _____

    b. What does the phrase mean in this story? _____

    c. Which words in the story give you the best clue about the real meaning of the phrase? _____

- No matter what we do or say, we can't get Annie to smile. She looks so unhappy since her best friend moved to another town. I guess it will take a while before she stops **feeling blue**.

    a. Without the story, what do the words in the highlighted phrase seem to be saying? _____

    b. What does the phrase mean in this story? _____

    c. Which words in the story give you the best clue about the real meaning of the phrase? _____

HIGHLIGHTED IDIOMS

1. Steve is a really great guy. Anytime you need help, he's ready to do more than his share. He's always willing to give you money if you're not able to pay your bills. There is nothing he won't do to help a friend. Why, he'd give you **the shirt off his back.**

   a. Without the story, what does the highlighted phrase appear to be saying?

   _____

   _____

   b. What does the phrase mean in this story? _____

   _____

   c. Which words in the story give you the best clue about the real meaning of the phrase?_____

   _____

2. I hate working with Barney. Whenever he talks, he mumbles his words or talks so softly I can hardly hear him. I messed up our last project together because his directions were **as clear as mud.**

   a. Without the story, what does the highlighted phrase appear to be saying?

   _____

   b. What does the phrase mean in this story? _____

   _____

   c. Which words in the story give you the best clue about the real meaning of the phrase?_____

   _____

3. Tommy had everything ready to plant the Smith's new garden. He was impatient to begin. Since Tommy and the Smiths hadn't had a chance to discuss just when he could start the job, he would have to wait for Mr. or Mrs. Smith to **give him the green light.**

   a. Without the story, what does the highlighted phrase appear to be saying?_____

   _____

   b. What does the phrase mean in this story? _____

   _____

   c. Which words in the story give you the best clue about the real meaning of the phrase?_____

   d. Can you think of another idiom that means the same thing? _____

   _____

HIGHLIGHTED IDIOMS

4. When I went to the beach last week, I dropped my contact lens in the sand. I searched and searched, but no luck! The tiny lens blended in so well with the sand I couldn't see it at all. I was **looking for a needle in a haystack.**

   a. Without the story, what does the highlighted phrase appear to be saying? _____

   b. What does the phrase mean in this story? _____

   c. Which words in the story give you the best clue about the real meaning of the phrase? _____

5. I didn't take the time to figure out how many sandwiches we'll need for the picnic because several people haven't let us know whether they're coming. **Off the top of my head,** I'd say 25 should be enough.

   a. Without the story, what does the highlighted phrase appear to be saying?

   _____

   _____

   b. What does the phrase mean in this story? _____

   _____

   c. Which words in the story give you the best clue about the real meaning of the phrase? _____

6. There is so much work to do in this old house. If we're going to move in by the end of the week, we have to scrub the floors, remove the old wallpaper and paint the bedrooms, clean the windows, and scour the kitchen and bathrooms. So **roll up your sleeves** and let's get busy!

   a. Without the story, what does the highlighted phrase appear to be saying?

   _____

   _____

   b. What does the phrase mean in this story? _____

   _____

   c. Which words in the story give you the best clue about the real meaning of the phrase? _____

HIGHLIGHTED IDIOMS

7. I wish you wouldn't keep interrupting me. Just when I know what I want to say, you mention some other topic and make me **lose my train of thought**. What was I talking about?

   a. Without the story, what does the highlighted phrase appear to be saying?
   _____
   _____

   b. What does the highlighted phrase mean in this story? _____
   _____

   c. Which words in the story give you the best clue about the real meaning of the phrase?_____

8. When I told the decorating committee how I planned to put rainbow-colored balloons and ribbons all over the gym, they were very excited. They **turned thumbs up** on my idea and gave me enough money to buy everything I needed.

   a. Without the story, what does the highlighted phrase appear to be saying?
   _____
   _____

   b. What does the phrase mean in this story? _____
   _____

   c. Which words in the story give you the best clue about the real meaning of the phrase?_____

   d. What would *turn thumbs down* mean?_____

9. Miyako tried on her wedding gown. It looked wonderful! All the wedding plans were going very well, and their honeymoon in Hawaii was all arranged. She was **on cloud nine**.

   a. Without the story, what does the highlighted phrase appear to be saying?
   _____

   b. What does the phrase mean in this story? _____
   _____

   c. Which words in the story give you the best clue about the real meaning of the phrase?_____
   _____

HIGHLIGHTED IDIOMS

10. It's fun to have an all-girl party. We tell each other things we don't want to discuss with our parents or when boys are around. It feels good to be able to say just about anything without feeling like a jerk. When else can you really **let your hair down** and tell all?

    a. Without the story, what does the highlighted phrase appear to be saying?

    _____

    _____

    b. What does the phrase mean in this story? _____

    _____

    c. Which words in the story give you the best clue about the real meaning of the phrase? _____

11. It looks like another hurricane is headed toward our town by tomorrow evening. Take all proper hurricane precautions. Remember to board up windows, have flashlights handy, and have enough food and water available for several days. **You know the drill.**

    a. Without the story, what does the highlighted phrase appear to be saying?

    _____

    _____

    b. What does the phrase mean in this story? _____

    _____

    c. Which words in the story give you the best clue about the real meaning of the phrase? _____

12. When Mom and Dad divorced, I was told I would have to choose which one I wanted to live with. I love them both. How can I possibly choose? I'm really **between a rock and a hard place.**

    a. Without the story, what does the highlighted phrase appear to be saying?

    _____

    _____

    b. What does the phrase mean in this story? _____

    _____

    c. Which words in the story give you the best clue about the real meaning of the phrase? _____

    _____

PARAGRAPH WITH MULTIPLE MEANING WORDS AND PHRASES

DIRECTIONS

The highlighted (bold-faced) words and phrases in this paragraph can have more than one meaning. Figure out what they mean here, and retell the story in your own words.

Since he'd been **fired** off the **city force** six months before, things hadn't been going so well. Mike wasn't complaining. A cop has to **keep his head**, and **he'd lost his**. But when you catch a crummy **pusher breaking in kids on the stuff**—well, it's pretty easy to **blow your top**. The **papers** had demanded the **riddance** of a brutal, sadistic cop. He **hadn't had a leg to stand on**. The chief had said, "Sorry, Mike. Maybe later, when this **blows over**." But Mike knew better than that. Still, the chief and Rogers had **plugged him** for this chance. He was grateful. And Rogers had said, "This could be **your big break**, Mike. Do a good job **down there**, make friends, and you'll be **fixed for life**."

HIGHLIGHTED WORDS	MEANING
fired	_____
city force	_____
keep his head	_____
he'd lost his	_____
pusher	_____
breaking in kids on the stuff	_____
blow your top	_____
papers	_____
riddance	_____
hadn't had a leg to stand on	_____
blows over	_____
plugged him	_____
your big break	_____
down there	_____
fixed for life	_____

Saying One Thing, Meaning Another

PARAGRAPHS FROM A TEEN MAGAZINE

DIRECTIONS

Underline the phrases in the following paragraphs that can be taken in two ways. Rewrite the paragraphs to make their real meaning clear.

A. "When you want to go four-wheeling on the beach, don't take your dad along to ride shotgun. Make sure you're up for this kind of a ride—remember, you want to keep the beach happy (respect the earth kind of thing). Also remember to check with the main dude-in-blue for the latest scoop on beach driving, and then go for it!"

_____

_____

_____

_____

_____

_____

_____

B. "I couldn't decide whether I wanted to continue staring into his baby blues, or head on out for some Buffalo wings, fries, and something wet. The ol' tummy rumbles were setting in fast and furious."

_____

_____

_____

_____

_____

_____

_____

IDIOMS

DIRECTIONS

Each of the following items contains a phrase, usually an idiomatic expression, that does not mean exactly what it appears to be saying. Some idioms can be figured out by looking at the thought expressed by the words in the phrase, but some cannot. Try to figure out the meanings of these phrases. Complete the examples below with someone. Be sure to use any clues you can find. Then figure out the meanings of the phrases on the activity pages that follow.

- Amy: "My baby sister learned how to put out the candles on her birthday cake."
  Nancy: "I know. Your mother gave me a blow-by-blow description."

    a. Which phrase did Nancy use that can be taken in two ways?
    _____

    b. What did Nancy mean? _____
    _____

    c. What else can it mean? _____
    _____

    d. Which words give the best clue for Nancy's interpretation? _____
    _____

- Barbara: "Why are vampires so unpopular?"
  Larry: "Because they're a pain in the neck."

    a. Which phrase in Larry's answer can be taken in two ways?
    _____

    b. What does Larry mean? _____

    c. What else could the phrase mean? _____
    _____

    d. Which word gives the best clue for Larry's meaning? _____
    _____

    e. Which word gives the best clue for the real meaning of the idiom?
    _____

IDIOMS I

1. Rose: "I'm so annoyed with Joe. I asked him to give me a hand after I slipped on the ice."
   Lily: "Why are you annoyed?"
   Rose: "He stood there and applauded."

   a. Which phrase in Rose's first comment can be taken in two ways?
   _____

   b. What did Rose mean? _____

   c. How did Joe interpret it? _____

   d. Which word gives you a clue for Joe's interpretation? _____
   _____

2. The fortune teller said she liked her work because she always had a ball.

   a. Which phrase in this joke can be taken in two ways? _____
   _____

   b. What are the two meanings? _____
   _____

   c. Which words in this joke give you a clue for one of the meanings?
   _____

3. Humpty Dumpty is just a shell of his former self.

   a. Which phrase in this joke can be taken in two ways? _____
   _____

   b. What does it mean here? _____

   c. What else can it mean? _____

   d. Which words in the comment give you a clue for the first meaning?
   _____

4. Q. Why did Snoopy want to quit the comic strip?
   A. He was tired of working for Peanuts.

   a. Which phrase in the answer can be used in two ways?
   _____

   b. What does it mean here? _____

   c. What else can it mean? _____

   d. Which words in the riddle give you a clue for the first meaning?
   _____

IDIOMS I

5. Look at the cartoon.

"GOSH. YOU REALLY DO EAT LIKE A BIRD."

© 1984 by Charles Almon. Reprinted with permission.

a. Which expression in the caption of this cartoon can be taken in two ways? _____

b. What does it mean in this cartoon? _____

c. What else can it mean? _____

d. What do you see in the cartoon that gives you a clue for the first meaning? _____

6. Look at the cartoon.

a. Which phrase in this advertisement can be taken in two ways? _____

b. What does it mean here? _____

c. What else can it mean? _____

d. What do you see in the cartoon that gives you a clue for the first meaning? _____

144   *Saying One Thing, Meaning Another*   © 1997 CC Spector. Published by Super Duper® Publications. Duplication permitted for educational use only.

IDIOMS 1

7. Sign in a music store window:

> # COME IN, PICK OUT A DRUM, THEN BEAT IT

   a. Which phrase on this sign can be taken in two ways? _____
   _____

   b. What does it mean here? _____

   c. What else can it mean? _____

   d. Which word in the sign gives you a clue for the first meaning?
   _____

8. Rich went to a hot dog stand and ordered a frankfurter from the bottom of the pile. "No problem," said the vendor, "But how come?" Rich explained, "I'm always for the underdog."

   a. Which phrase in this joke can be taken in two ways? _____
   _____

   b. What did Rich mean? _____

   c. What else can it mean? _____

   d. Which words in the joke give you a clue for the first meaning?
   _____

9. Look at the cartoon.

   a. Which phrase in this cartoon can be used in two ways? _____
   _____

   b. What does it mean here? _____
   _____

   c. What else can it mean? _____
   _____

   d. What do you see in the cartoon that gives you a clue to each meaning? _____
   _____

IDIOMS I   10. Look at the cartoon.

a. Which phrase in this comic strip can be used in two ways? _____
_____

b. What does it mean here? _____
_____

c. What else can it mean? _____
_____

d. What do you see in the cartoon that gives you a clue for the first meaning? _____
_____

IDIOMS II

1. Q. Why don't skeletons ski?
   A. They don't have the guts.

   a. Which phrase in the answer can be used in two ways? _____
   _____

   b. What does it mean here? _____

   c. What else can it mean? _____

   d. Which word in the question gives you a clue for the first meaning?
   _____

2. Alfie: "Did you hear about the robbery on the clothesline?"
   Mollie: "No. What happened?"
   Alfie: "Two clothespins held up a pair of pants."

   a. Which phrase in Alfie's answer can be taken in two ways? _____
   _____

   b. What does it mean here? _____

   c. What else can it mean? _____

   d. Which words in Alfie's question and answer give you clues to each
      meaning? _____

3. My electrician is always worrying about current events.

   a. Which phrase in this joke can be taken in two ways? _____
   _____

   b. What does it mean here? _____

   c. What else can it mean? _____

   d. Which word in the joke gives you a clue for the first meaning?
   _____

4. I can tell my pet owl is sick because he doesn't give a hoot.

   a. Which phrase in this joke can be taken in two ways? _____
   _____

   b. What does it mean here? _____

   c. What else can it mean? _____

   d. Which word in the joke gives you a clue for the first meaning?
   _____

Chapter 5

IDIOMS II

5. Look at the cartoon.

DEBTS PILING UP?
IF IT'S TIME TO PAY THE PIPER, WE CAN HELP.
ACME LOAN AGENCY.

a. Which phrase in this cartoon caption can be used in two ways? _____

b. What does it mean here? _____

c. What else can it mean? _____

d. Which words in the cartoon caption give you a clue for the second meaning? _____

6. Look at the cartoon.

"Billy's not very nice. He told me to break a leg."

© 1994 by King Features Syndicate. Reprinted with special permission.

a. Which phrase in this cartoon caption can be taken in two ways? _____

b. What does the little girl think it means? _____

c. What did Billy really mean? _____

d. What do you see in the cartoon that gives you clues for what Billy meant? _____

148 Saying One Thing, Meaning Another

IDIOMS II

7. When the first automatic packaging machine was invented, the inventor made a bundle.

    a. Which phrase in this joke can be taken in two ways? _____
    _____

    b. What does it mean here? _____

    c. What else can it mean? _____

    d. Which word in the joke gives you a clue for the first meaning?
    _____

8. Q. What does a worm in a cornfield do?
   A. It goes in one ear and out the other.

    a. Which phrase in this riddle can be used in two ways? _____
    _____

    b. What does the answer mean in this riddle? _____
    _____

    c. What else can the answer mean? _____

    d. Which word in the riddle gives you a clue for the first meaning?
    _____

9. Look at the cartoon.

ON SALE NOW AT YOUR LOCAL BOOKSTORE.

    a. Which expression in this cartoon can be used in two ways? _____
    _____

    b. What does it mean according to the book cover illustration? _____
    _____
    _____

    c. What does it really mean? _____
    _____
    _____

    d. What do you see in the cartoon that gives you a clue for each of the meanings? _____
    _____
    _____

IDIOMS II

10 Look at the cartoon.

Hey, c'mon now!...
You two were made for each other!

a. Which phrase in this cartoon caption can be taken in two ways? _____

b. What does it mean here? _____

c. What else can it mean? _____

d. What do you see in the cartoon that gives you clues for the first meaning? _____

IDIOMS III

1. Q. Why did the orange stop in the middle of the road?
   A. It ran out of juice.

   a. Which phrase in this riddle can be used in two ways? _____
   _____

   b. What does it mean here? _____

   c. What else can it mean? _____

   d. Which words in the question give you a clue for the second meaning?
   _____

2. Look at the cartoon.

   "I'm sitting on top of the world in my Celeste Bridal Gown!"

   a. Which phrase in this cartoon can be used in two ways? _____
   _____

   b. How is it used in this cartoon? _____
   _____
   _____

   c. What does it really mean? _____
   _____
   _____

   d. What do you see in the cartoon that gives you a clue for the real meaning? _____
   _____
   _____

3. When the first credit card was invented, people got a charge out of it.

   a. Which phrase in this joke can be taken in two ways? _____
   _____

   b. What does it mean here? _____

   c. What else can it mean? _____

   d. Which words in the joke give you a clue for the second meaning?
   _____

IDIOMS III

4. Look at the cartoon.

    a. Which phrase in this cartoon can be taken in two ways? _____
_____

    b. What does it mean here? _____

    c. What else can it mean? _____

    d. What do you see in the cartoon that gives you a clue for the first meaning? _____
_____

5. Look at the cartoon.

"WHY DID YOU PUT THEM ALL IN ONE BASKET?"

    a. On which expression is this cartoon caption based? _____
_____

    b. What does it mean? _____
_____
_____

    c. What do you see in the cartoon that gives you a clue for the real meaning? _____
_____
_____

Saying One Thing, Meaning Another

IDIOMS III

6. Look at the cartoon.

YOU WON'T HAVE TO PAY AN ARM AND A LEG FOR A NEW CAR. COME IN AND ASK ABOUT OUR LOW, LOW PRICES!

   a. Which phrase in this cartoon caption can be used in two ways?
   _____

   b. What does it mean here? _____

   c. What does it really mean? _____

   d. Which words in the cartoon caption give you a clue for the real meaning?
   _____

7. Look at the cartoon.

   a. Which phrase on this greeting card can be used in two ways? _____

   b. What does it mean here? _____

   c. What does it really mean? _____

   d. What do you see in the cartoon that gives you a clue for the real meaning? _____

IDIOMS III

8. Look at the cartoon.

HOLIER THAN THOU.

a. What does *holier than thou* mean in this cartoon? _____

b. What does it really mean? _____

c. What do you see in the cartoon that gives you a clue for the real meaning? _____

9. Look at the cartoon.

"...and this must be the little woman."

© 1980. The Far Side cartoon by Gary Larson is reprinted by permission of Chronicle Features, San Francisco, CA. All rights reserved.

a. Which phrase in this cartoon caption can be used in two ways? _____

b. What does it mean here? _____

c. What else can it mean? _____

d. What do you see in the cartoon that gives you a clue for the first meaning? _____

e. Can you think of any reason why women would object to this cartoon? _____

IDIOMS III

10. "What was your profession?" asked the cannibal chief. "I was an editor of a newspaper." "Good," said the chief with a smile. "Tomorrow you will be editor-in-chief."

   a. Which phrase in this joke is being used in two ways? _____

   _____

   b. What does it mean here? _____

   c. What else can it mean? _____

   d. Which word in the joke gives you a clue for one of the meanings?

   _____

IDIOMS IV

1. Idioms often are heard in movies and television programs. The idioms mentioned below were heard in a "Star Trek" movie. Figure out their meanings.

   a. "Stuck between a rock and a hard place" _____
   _____

   b. Mr. Spock: "I'm all ears" _____

   c. "Take it from the top" _____

   d. "Take your best shot" _____

   e. Referring to the starship Enterprise: "Let's see what she's got"
   _____

2. Look at the cartoon.

© 1994 by King Features Syndicate. Reprinted with special permission.

   a. Which phrase in the cartoon can be used in two ways? _____
   _____

   b. What does Hagar mean when he says "look out for number one"?
   _____

   c. What does his companion take it to mean? _____
   _____

   d. What do you see in the comic strip that gives you a clue for what Hagar meant? _____

156 | *Saying One Thing, Meaning Another* © 1997 CC Spector. Published by Super Duper® Publications. Duplication permitted for educational use only.

IDIOMS IV

3. Look at the cartoon.

© 1984 by Tribune Media Services. Reprinted with permission.

   a. Which phrase in this comic strip is being used in two ways? _____
   _____

   b. What does the Reverend think the woman means? _____
   _____

   c. What does she really mean? _____
   _____

   d. What do you see in the comic strip that gives you a clue for what the woman means? _____

4. Look at the cartoon.

   a. Which phrase in this cartoon caption can be taken in two ways? _____
   _____

   b. How is it being used here? _____
   _____
   _____

   c. What does it really mean? _____
   _____
   _____

   d. What do you see in the cartoon that gives you a clue for the first meaning? _____
   _____
   _____

IDIOMS IV

5. Look at the cartoon.

a. Which expression in the man's thoughts can be taken in two ways? _____

b. What does he mean? _____

c. What else can it mean? _____

d. Which expression in the woman's thoughts can be taken in two ways? _____

e. What does she mean? _____

f. What else can it mean? _____

g. What does the cartoon caption lead you to believe? _____

6. Look at the cartoon.

a. Which phrase in this comic strip can be used in two ways?

_____

158 | Saying One Thing, Meaning Another

IDIOMS IV

b. What does "Soup to Nuts" mean on the sign? _____
_____

c. What does Roz say it means? _____

d. What does Roz say that offers you a clue for what she means? _____
_____

7. Look at the cartoon.

a. Which comment made by the baby on the left can be taken in two ways? _____
_____

b. What does the baby mean? _____
_____

c. What else could it mean? _____
_____

d. Which comment made by the baby on the right can be taken in two ways? _____
_____
_____

e. What does the baby mean? _____
_____

f. What else could it mean? _____
_____
_____

g. Which comment made by the baby in the middle can be taken in two ways? _____
_____

h. What does the baby mean? _____
_____

i. What else could it mean? _____
_____

j. Which meanings are appropriate for the cartoon caption? _____
_____
_____

IDIOMS IV

8. Two of the clocks in the cartoon below bring to mind common expressions. One starts with "Quick" and the other with "Slow." Examine the clocks very carefully to figure out these expressions.

a. "Quick as _____"

b. "Slow as _____"

c. What do you see in the cartoon that gives you clues? _____
_____
_____

Saying One Thing, Meaning Another

MATCHING INDIVIDUALS WITH THE APPROPRIATE "COMPLIMENTS"

DIRECTIONS

Match the individual in column I to the "compliment" in column II, and then state the real meaning of the phrase. Explain why the "compliment" is appropriate for each individual.

I	II
1. Frankenstein _____	A. faultless
2. ET _____	B. well groomed
3. Wyatt Earp _____	C. levelheaded
4. Tennis champion _____	D. down to earth
5. Man married 5 times _____	E. straight shooter

REAL MEANING

A. _____

B. _____

C. _____

D. _____

E. _____

WHY IS THE COMPLIMENT APPROPRIATE?

1. _____

2. _____

3. _____

4. _____

5. _____

IDIOMS AND PROVERBS FROM OTHER COUNTRIES

DID YOU KNOW...

A *proverb* is an expression that provides a moral lesson, a bit of advice on how to act or think. Like idioms, the words can be taken literally or figuratively. For example, the proverb *Don't put all your eggs in one basket* can be taken literally to mean that if you are gathering eggs, don't place them all in one basket, or figuratively to mean that you shouldn't place all your hopes or efforts into one venture.

DIRECTIONS

In this activity, we will look at the figurative meaning of some proverbs and idioms. In other countries, the thoughts conveyed by American idioms and proverbs are expressed differently. Try to match the American expressions in column I with the foreign expressions in column II that convey the same sentiment, and figure out what they mean. Use an idiom or proverb dictionary when necessary.

I	II
1. A drop in the bucket _____	A. There are no waves if there is no wind
2. As ye sow, so shall ye reap _____	B. When you speak of teao teao, teao teao arrives
3. Picky, picky, picky _____	C. Riding a tiger and finding it hard to get off
4. One rotten apple spoils the barrel _____	D. To blow on the hair and search for tiny sores
5. It takes two to tango _____	E. The horse that leads the herd astray
6. Like comparing apples and oranges _____	F. Paper cannot wrap up fire
7. Speak of the devil _____	G. One hair from nine oxen
8. Where there's smoke, there's fire _____	H. The mouth of the cow does not fit the head of the horse
9. Building castles in the air _____	I. If one plants melons, one gets melons
10. Biting off more than you can chew _____	J. It is impossible to clap with only one hand

Discuss with others: Why is it helpful to understand foreign expressions?

IDIOMS THAT MEAN THE SAME THING

DIRECTIONS

Sometimes two idioms have the same meaning even though they are made up of different words. Find a definition for each pair of idioms. Use an idiom dictionary if necessary.

Example: fly off the handle/lose one's temper
Definition: to become very angry, to lose control

1. Close up shop/Call it a day
   Definition: _____

2. Give the cold shoulder/Look down one's nose at
   Definition: _____

3. Every which way/Helter-skelter
   Definition: _____

4. Hem and haw/Beat around the bush
   Definition: _____

5. Hit the ceiling/Blow a fuse
   Definition: _____

6. Give up/Throw in the towel
   Definition: _____

7. Lose one's self/In a world of one's own
   Definition: _____

8. Leave high and dry/Leave in the lurch
   Definition: _____

9. Beside the point/Neither here nor there
   Definition: _____

10. Life of Riley/Bed of roses
    Definition: _____

11. Month of Sundays/In a dog's age
    Definition: _____

12. Dot the i's and cross the t's/Mind one's p's and q's
    Definition: _____

IDIOMS AND PROVERBS WITH OPPOSITE MEANINGS

DID YOU KNOW...

At times, the thought expressed by one idiom or proverb may be exactly the opposite of the thought expressed by another. For example, a bald man may say, "Grass doesn't grow on a busy street." A man with a full head of hair may respond, "There's no sense in putting a roof on an empty shed." The bald man is saying that he's using his head (thinking) so much that hair can't put down roots and grow there. The man with lots of hair is saying that if nothing is inside your head (like brains), then you don't need anything to cover it up.

DIRECTIONS

Find the meanings for the following opposing pairs of idioms and proverbs. Write the meanings after each pair.

1. Open-and-shut case/No leg to stand on

   Meanings: _____
   _____

2. What you see is what you get/Don't judge a book by its cover

   Meanings: _____
   _____

3. Many hands make light work/Too many cooks spoil the broth

   Meanings: _____
   _____

4. Pinch pennies/Easy come, easy go

   Meanings: _____
   _____

5. Hold the fort/Give up (give in)

   Meanings: _____
   _____

6. Perish the thought/Keep that in mind

   Meanings: _____
   _____

IDIOMS AND PROVERBS WITH OPPOSITE MEANINGS

7. Pull the wool over one's eyes/Be up front

   Meanings: _____

   _____

8. Hold up/Fall apart

   Meanings: _____

   _____

9. Fall short/Measure up

   Meanings: _____

   _____

10. Absence makes the heart grow fonder/Out of sight, out of mind

    Meanings: _____

    _____

11. He who hesitates is lost/Look before you leap

    Meanings: _____

    _____

12. Two is company, three's a crowd/The more, the merrier

    Meanings: _____

    _____

IDIOMS WITH ONLY A FIGURATIVE MEANING

DID YOU KNOW...

Some idioms can be used only in the figurative sense, for example, "I see my old friend Joe *once in a blue moon*." Figuratively, *once in a blue moon* means very rarely or almost never. It is not possible to interpret this expression literally in a generally accepted sense.

DIRECTIONS

Use an idiom dictionary to determine the meaning of the idioms that follow. Use each one in a sentence.

1. All kidding aside

    Meaning: _____

    Sentence: _____

    _____

2. Armed to the teeth

    Meaning: _____

    Sentence: _____

    _____

3. Beat the rap

    Meaning: _____

    Sentence: _____

    _____

4. Bread-and-butter letter

    Meaning: _____

    Sentence: _____

    _____

5. By the skin of one's teeth

    Meaning: _____

    Sentence: _____

    _____

IDIOMS WITH ONLY A FIGURATIVE MEANING

6. Fall in love

   Meaning: _____

   Sentence:_____

   _____

7. On the spur of the moment

   Meaning: _____

   Sentence:_____

   _____

8. Throw a party

   Meaning: _____

   Sentence:_____

   _____

9. Born with a silver spoon in one's mouth

   Meaning: _____

   Sentence:_____

   _____

10. Catch cold

    Meaning: _____

    Sentence:_____

    _____

11. Doesn't add up to a hill of beans

    Meaning: _____

    Sentence:_____

    _____

12. Make good time

    Meaning: _____

    Sentence:_____

    _____

FIXED-ORDER IDIOMS

DIRECTIONS

Some phrases in the English language are always said in the same order. For example, we say *salt and pepper* and *up and down*, and not *pepper and salt* or *down and up*. The following fixed-order idioms in column I are defined in column II. Write the letter for the correct definition next to each idiom.

I	II
1. sick and tired _____	A. that famous and talented person; a person's spouse
2. pick and choose _____	B. absolutely without further complication or elaboration
3. good and ready _____	C. having no money or means of support
4. one and only _____	D. select with much care; take a long time before choosing
5. rough and ready _____	E. strong, active, and ready for anything
6. leave someone high and dry _____	F. abandon someone; leave one helpless
7. mind your p's and q's _____	G. sneaky, unfair, low-down, nasty
8. plain and simple _____	H. feeling well; healthy
9. down and dirty _____	I. use your best manners; be careful, thorough
10. down and out _____	J. do something only when you want to and not before
11. alive and kicking _____	K. very uncertain or critical
12. touch and go _____	L. very annoyed about; feeling strong dislike for something repeated or continued too long

Saying One Thing, Meaning Another © 1997 CC Spector. Published by Super Duper® Publications. Duplication permitted for educational use only.

MORE FIXED-ORDER IDIOMS

DIRECTIONS

Match the fixed-order idioms in column I with their definitions in column II. Write the letter for the correct definition next to each idiom. Then look at the cartoon on the next page, which contains a fixed-order idiom. Use the visual clues to figure out the idiom's meaning.

I	II
1. in black and white _____	A. flexibility; willingness to compromise
2. free and easy _____	B. official; in writing
3. live and learn _____	C. to endure something unpleasant in good humor
4. give-and-take _____	D. casual
5. grin and bear it _____	E. regular soldiers; not the officers
6. quick and dirty _____	F. comparing two things that are not really similar
7. rank and file _____	G. increase one's knowledge by experience
8. apples and oranges _____	H. capture and release someone over and over; tease
9. play cat and mouse _____	I. done fast and carelessly

MORE FIXED-ORDER IDIOMS

10. Look at the cartoon.

© 1990 by King Features Syndicate. Reprinted with special permission.

a. What does *six of one and a half a dozen of the other* mean in this cartoon?
_____
_____

b. What does it mean in general? _____
_____
_____

c. What do you see in the cartoon that gives you a clue? _____
_____
_____

IDIOMS AND PHRASES WITH THREE WORDS IN FIXED ORDER

DIRECTIONS

Some idioms and phrases contain three words that are always in a fixed order. As in two-word fixed-order idioms or phrases, *and* or *or* are the connector words. The words in these idioms or phrases are used only in the sequences shown. Match the idioms in column I with their definitions in column II. Write the letter for the correct definition next to each idiom.

I	II
1. between you, me, and the lamppost _____	A. everyone without discrimination
2. blood, sweat, and tears _____	B. formally and officially signed
3. coffee, tea, or milk _____	C. eager or at least willing to do something
4. fold, spindle, or mutilate _____	D. everything
5. a hop, skip, and a jump _____	E. without question or doubt; completely
6. lock, stock, and barrel _____	F. a choice of beverages on an airline
7. ready, willing, and able _____	G. symbols of witchcraft
8. signed, sealed, and delivered _____	H. the signs of great personal effort
9. every Tom, Dick, and Harry _____	I. to disfigure a machine-readable document
10. bell, book, and candle _____	J. exercise caution
11. hook, line, and sinker _____	K. secretively
12. stop, look, and listen _____	L. the American flag
13. the red, white, and blue _____	M. a short distance

FIXED-ORDER IDIOM DEFINITIONS 1

DIRECTIONS

Use an idiom dictionary to define these fixed-order idioms. Notice that *and* is the connector word in each of these phrases. Use each of these idioms in a sentence.

1. flora and fauna

    Definition: _____

    Sentence: _____

    _____

2. sticks and stones

    Definition: _____

    Sentence: _____

    _____

3. song and dance

    Definition: _____

    Sentence: _____

    _____

4. sweet and sour

    Definition: _____

    Sentence: _____

    _____

5. null and void

    Definition: _____

    Sentence: _____

    _____

6. trial and error

    Definition: _____

    Sentence: _____

    _____

FIXED-ORDER IDIOM DEFINITIONS I

7. wine and dine

    Definition: _____

    Sentence: _____

    _____

8. ups and downs

    Definition: _____

    Sentence: _____

    _____

9. spick-and-span

    Definition: _____

    Sentence: _____

    _____

10. stop-and-go

    Definition: _____

    Sentence: _____

    _____

11. straight and narrow

    Definition: _____

    Sentence: _____

    _____

12. odds and ends

    Definition: _____

    Sentence: _____

    _____

FIXED-ORDER IDIOM DEFINITIONS II

DIRECTIONS

Use an idiom dictionary to define these fixed-order idioms. Notice that *and* is the connector word in each of these phrases. Use each of these idioms in a sentence.

1. meat and potatoes

   Definition: _____

   Sentence: _____

   _____

2. bed-and-breakfast

   Definition: _____

   Sentence: _____

   _____

3. above and beyond

   Definition: _____

   Sentence: _____

   _____

4. now and then

   Definition: _____

   Sentence: _____

   _____

5. off and running

   Definition: _____

   Sentence: _____

   _____

6. nuts and bolts

   Definition: _____

   Sentence: _____

   _____

FIXED-ORDER IDIOM DEFINITIONS II

7. horse and buggy

   Definition: _____

   Sentence: _____

   _____

8. hot and cold

   Definition: _____

   Sentence: _____

   _____

9. hunt-and-peck

   Definition: _____

   Sentence: _____

   _____

10. live and let live

    Definition: _____

    Sentence: _____

    _____

11. hit-and-run

    Definition: _____

    Sentence: _____

    _____

12. fair and square

    Definition: _____

    Sentence: _____

    _____

FIXED-ORDER IDIOM DEFINITIONS III

DIRECTIONS

Use an idiom dictionary to define these fixed-order idioms. Notice that *and* is the connector word in each of these phrases. Use each of these idioms in a sentence.

1. far and wide

    Definition: _____

    Sentence: _____

    _____

2. few and far between

    Definition: _____

    Sentence: _____

    _____

3. fine and dandy

    Definition: _____

    Sentence: _____

    _____

4. hard-and-fast

    Definition: _____

    Sentence: _____

    _____

5. dead and buried

    Definition: _____

    Sentence: _____

    _____

6. ebb and flow

    Definition: _____

    Sentence: _____

    _____

FIXED-ORDER IDIOM DEFINITIONS III

7. bread and butter

   Definition: _____

   Sentence: _____

   _____

8. high and mighty

   Definition: _____

   Sentence: _____

   _____

9. tried-and-true

   Definition: _____

   Sentence: _____

   _____

10. pins and needles

    Definition: _____

    Sentence: _____

    _____

11. pros and cons

    Definition: _____

    Sentence: _____

    _____

12. bright and early

    Definition: _____

    Sentence: _____

    _____

FIXED-ORDER IDIOM DEFINITIONS IV

DIRECTIONS

Use an idiom dictionary to define the following fixed-order idioms. Notice that each of these phrases has *or* as the connector word. Use each of these idioms in a sentence.

1. shape up or ship out

    Definition: _____

    Sentence: _____

    _____

2. sooner or later

    Definition: _____

    Sentence: _____

    _____

3. sink or swim

    Definition: _____

    Sentence: _____

    _____

4. more or less

    Definition: _____

    Sentence: _____

    _____

5. now or never

    Definition: _____

    Sentence: _____

    _____

6. make or break

    Definition: _____

    Sentence: _____

    _____

FIXED-ORDER IDIOM DEFINITIONS IV

7. hit or miss

   Definition: _____

   Sentence: _____

   _____

8. feast or famine

   Definition: _____

   Sentence: _____

   _____

9. like it or lump it

   Definition: _____

   Sentence: _____

   _____

10. take it or leave it

    Definition: _____

    Sentence: _____

    _____

11. friend or foe

    Definition: _____

    Sentence: _____

    _____

12. right or wrong

    Definition: _____

    Sentence: _____

    _____

FIXED-ORDER IDIOM DEFINITIONS V

DIRECTIONS

Some idioms are made up of words that repeat themselves. Use an idiom dictionary to define the idioms that follow. Use each of these idioms in a sentence.

1. see eye to eye

    Definition: _____

    Sentence: _____

    _____

2. side by side

    Definition: _____

    Sentence: _____

    _____

3. door to door

    Definition: _____

    Sentence: _____

    _____

4. fifty-fifty

    Definition: _____

    Sentence: _____

    _____

5. arm in arm

    Definition: _____

    Sentence: _____

    _____

6. from hand to hand

    Definition: _____

    Sentence: _____

    _____

FIXED-ORDER IDIOM DEFINITIONS V

7. from time to time

    Definition: _____

    Sentence: _____

    _____

8. from day to day

    Definition: _____

    Sentence: _____

    _____

9. by and by

    Definition: _____

    Sentence: _____

    _____

10. share and share alike

    Definition: _____

    Sentence: _____

    _____

11. so-and-so

    Definition: _____

    Sentence: _____

    _____

12. half-and-half

    Definition: _____

    Sentence: _____

    _____

MULTIPLE MEANING PHRASE DRAWINGS

DIRECTIONS

This activity provides an enjoyable way to study yet another group of idioms and phrases. It uses a form of problem solving that focuses on visual clues. In the items that follow, a familiar idiom or phrase is formed by each group of letters. The arrangement of the letters is a clue to the idiom's meaning. Find the idiom or phrase "hidden" in each of the following word "drawings" and explain what it means. Complete the examples on this page with someone. Then figure out the phrases on the activity pages that follow. Use an idiom dictionary if necessary.

- he's/himself   It means _____
_____
_____
_____

- R   It means _____
  U   _____
    N   _____
_____

Saying One Thing, Meaning Another © 1997 CC Spector. Published by Super Duper® Publications. Duplication permitted for educational use only.

MULTIPLE MEANING PHRASE DRAWINGS I

1.   j

    you u me

        s

        t

    It means _____

    _____

    _____

    _____

2. your no no no

       right

    It means _____

    _____

    _____

    _____

    _____

3. m   e   a   l

    e   a

    a   e

    l   a   e   m

    It means _____

    _____

    _____

    _____

4. ground

    feet

    feet

    feet

    feet

    feet

    feet

    It means _____

    _____

    _____

5. LINES READ LINES

    It means _____

    _____

    _____

    _____

6. TOUKEEPCH

    It means _____

    _____

    _____

    _____

MULTIPLE MEANING PHRASE DRAWINGS I

7. Go
   forever

It means _____
_____
_____
_____

8. R
    E
    H
    L
    L
    I
    F

It means _____
_____
_____
_____

9. ONE   THE OTHER
   ONE   THE OTHER
   ONE   THE OTHER
   ONE   THE OTHER
   ONE   THE OTHER
   ONE   THE OTHER

It means _____
_____
_____
_____

10. E
     V
     I
     G

It means _____
_____
_____
_____

11. DEAL

It means _____
_____
_____
_____

12. The Bridge

    Water

It means _____
_____
_____
_____

Saying One Thing, Meaning Another   © 1997 CC Spector. Published by Super Duper® Publications. Duplication permitted for educational use only.

MULTIPLE MEANING PHRASE DRAWINGS II

1. Give her HAND   It means _____

2.   Go   It means _____

      Board

3.   SITTING   It means _____
      the fence

4. you can't have it   It means _____
   ti evah t'nac uoy

5.   D   It means _____
      E
      F

6. NEPAINCK   It means _____

MULTIPLE MEANING PHRASE DRAWINGS II

7. ONCE

    5:30

    It means _____
    _____
    _____
    _____

8. in

    my head

    It means _____
    _____
    _____
    _____

9. somedroptime

    It means _____
    _____
    _____
    _____

10. R
    E
    V
    O
    C

    It means _____
    _____
    _____
    _____

11. O

    N HIS LUCK

    It means _____
    _____
    _____
    _____

12. DRESSED KILL

    KILL

    It means _____
    _____
    _____
    _____

ADDITIONAL ACTIVITIES

1. Advise individuals to write down multiple meaning phrases heard in conversations, movies, television shows, etc. that are not understood. Encourage the use of idiom and proverb dictionaries. (See Appendix D for suggested texts.)

2. Ask individuals to write a paragraph using specified multiple meaning phrases. Discuss whether the context supports the phrases' intended meanings.

3. Use videotapes to present parts of movies or television shows. Help individuals recognize multiple meaning phrases as they occur.

4. Comedy routines often are based on ambiguous words and phrases. Show a videotape of a comedy routine and discuss the dual meanings of the words and phrases that cause the humor. Abbot and Costello's "Who's on First" routine is an excellent example, with words and phrases such as *who, what, I don't know, I don't give a darn, today,* and *tomorrow* being used as baseball players' names. (This routine can be found in the 1945 movie *The Naughty Nineties.*)

5. Ask individuals to underline or circle multiple meaning phrases in newspaper articles or magazine stories. Discuss the meanings of the underlined or circled phrases as they relate to the context of the reading material.

6. Encourage individuals to collect ambiguous phrases heard in conversations, movies, television shows, on the radio, etc. and seen in newspapers, magazines, textbooks, store signs, billboards, bumper stickers, tee shirts, commercials, etc. These phrases can then be discussed and interpreted appropriately.

CHAPTER 5 ANSWER KEY

These answers are merely guidelines. The facilitator can judge if the individual's responses are appropriate for each item.

HIGHLIGHTED IDIOMS

Examples:

- a. eating food generally given to horses, such as oats and hay, from a feedbag
  b. eating large amounts of food
  c. enough food for two people, and eat every bit of it

- a. touching something that is blue
  b. feeling sad
  c. can't get Annie to smile, looks so unhappy since her best friend moved to another town

1a. He'd take off his shirt and give it to you.
 b. to be very generous
 c. he's ready to do more than his share, always willing to give you money, there is nothing he won't do to help a friend

2a. unclear, hard to see through
 b. not understandable
 c. mumbles, talks so softly I can hardly hear him, messed up

3a. give him a light that is green
 b. to give someone the signal to begin or continue
 c. just when he could start the job
 d. give (him) the go-ahead

4a. looking for a tiny sewing needle in a big pile of hay
 b. looking for anything that is hard to find
 c. blended in so well with the sand I couldn't see it at all

5a. something was sitting on her head and is now being removed
 b. to state something rapidly and without really thinking too long
 c. didn't take the time to figure out

6a. turn the cuffs up on your sleeves
 b. prepare to start working
 c. so much work to do, if we're going to move in by the end of the week (we must do all these jobs)

7a. lose a train that carries thought
 b. to forget what one was just talking or thinking about
 c. What was I talking about?

CHAPTER 5 ANSWER KEY

8a. put their thumbs up in the air
 b. to approve or accept something
 c. they were very excited, gave me enough money to buy everything I needed
 d. to disapprove or reject something

9a. sitting on a cloud
 b. very happy, too happy to think of anything else
 c. all the wedding plans were going very well

10a. take out all pins, barrettes, combs, etc., and let one's hair fall loose
 b. to become very intimate and begin to speak frankly, act freely and naturally, be informal
 c. to be able to say just about anything without feeling like a jerk (foolish)

11a. you are familiar with the drill (tool)
 b. you know what steps to take in this situation
 c. another hurricane is headed toward our town (you've been through this before)

12a. standing between a rock and another place that is hard
 b. in a very difficult position, facing a hard decision
 c. I would have to choose which one I wanted to live with, I love them both

PARAGRAPH WITH MULTIPLE MEANING WORDS AND PHRASES

fired—discharged, dismissed, let go

city force—city police department

keep his head—remain calm and sensible when in an awkward or troublesome situation that might cause a person to panic

he'd lost his (head)—became confused or acted irrationally

pusher—someone who sells illegal drugs

breaking in kids on the stuff—getting children started in the use of addictive drugs

blow your top—become very excited, angry, hysterical, or furious

papers—newspaper stories

riddance—get free of, relief from

hadn't had a leg to stand on—no firm foundation of facts, no facts to support a claim

blows over—goes away without causing harm, comes to an end

plugged him—picked him for the job, put him in the job

your big break—your chance, a stroke of good luck

down there—at a different (probably geographically more southern) location

fixed for life—be in a secure, comfortable financial position

CHAPTER 5 ANSWER KEY

Since he'd been dismissed from the city police department six months before, things hadn't been going so well. Mike wasn't complaining. A cop has to remain calm and sensible, and he had acted irrationally. But when you catch someone who sells illegal drugs to children, with the aim of getting them addicted—well, it's pretty easy to act in an irrational, angry manner. The newspaper stories had demanded they get rid of a brutal, sadistic cop. He had no way to show that he was justified in the way he had acted. The chief had said, "Sorry, Mike. Maybe later, when no more attention is given to this situation." But Mike knew better than that. Still, the chief and Rogers had picked him for this job. He was grateful. And Rogers had said, "This could be a stroke of good luck, Mike. Do a good job at your new location, make friends, and you'll be in a secure, comfortable financial position."

PARAGRAPHS FROM A TEEN MAGAZINE

A. four-wheeling
ride shotgun
you're up
keep the beach happy
respect the earth kind of thing
check with the main dude-in-blue
scoop
go for it

"When you drive a four-wheel vehicle on the beach, don't take your dad along to advise and protect you. Make sure you're ready to do this type of driving—remember, you don't want to damage the beach by mishandling your vehicle. Also remember to find out from the police chief what the current regulations are for beach driving before you start, and then go ahead and drive!"

B. baby blues
head on out
Buffalo wings
fries
something wet
ol' tummy rumbles
setting in
fast and furious

"I couldn't decide whether I wanted to continue staring into his blue eyes, or leave so I could get some chicken wings, prepared 'Buffalo' style, French fried potatoes, and a beverage. I was feeling very hungry, and my stomach was making more and more of the noises caused by emptiness."

CHAPTER 5 ANSWER KEY

IDIOMS

Examples:

- a. blow-by-blow
  b. described each puff of air
  c. describing every little detail
  d. put out the candles on her birthday cake

- a. pain in the neck
  b. They hurt you, because vampires bite your neck to drink your blood
  c. an annoying person
  d. vampires
  e. unpopular

IDIOMS I

1a. give me a hand
  b. help me
  c. clap for her
  d. applauded

2a. had a ball
  b. enjoyed herself, owned a crystal ball
  c. fortune-teller

3a. just a shell of his former self
  b. no egg inside
  c. not the way he used to be
  d. Humpty Dumpty (a nursery rhyme character that is an egg which falls and breaks)

4a. working for Peanuts
  b. working for the Peanuts comic strip
  c. working for very little money
  d. Snoopy, Peanuts

5a. eat like a bird
  b. bend one's head and body down and peck at the food the way a bird does
  c. eat very small portions at one time
  d. The woman is dressed in a way that makes her look like she has bird feathers, and she is pecking at the food.

6a. sitting pretty
  b. looking beautiful while sitting on a pretty sofa
  c. to be in a lucky position, living in comfort or luxury
  d. a pretty woman sitting on a nice new sofa

CHAPTER 5
ANSWER KEY

7a. beat it
 b. beat the drum
 c. go away, leave the vicinity of this store
 d. drum

8a. for the underdog
 b. He prefers the hot dog on the bottom.
 c. for the weaker person or weaker side in a match
 d. hot dog, bottom of the pile

9a. off the wall
 b. paint can be used on furniture and floors, not just walls
 c. odd, silly, unusual
 d. the floor and a chair are being painted and these items are somewhat unusual

10a. fast foods
 b. a fast-running animal that is considered food
 c. food that is already prepared or prepared in a very short time
 d. the animal is running very fast

IDIOMS II

1a. don't have the guts
 b. internal organs of the body
 c. do not have the courage
 d. skeletons

2a. held up
 b. kept fastened to the clothesline
 c. to rob
 d. robbery, clothespins

3a. current events
 b. electrical power, getting a shock
 c. what is happening in the world, news on television, newspapers, and so forth
 d. electrician

4a. doesn't give a hoot
 b. doesn't make a sound
 c. doesn't care
 d. The owl is sick.

5a. pay the piper
 b. give money to a person playing the bagpipes
 c. to face the results of your actions
 d. debts piling up

CHAPTER 5
ANSWER KEY

6a. break a leg
   b. fracture her leg
   c. good luck (especially in the theatrical business)
   d. little girl is wearing a ballet costume, and the sign says "Dance recital"

7a. made a bundle
   b. made a package
   c. made a lot of money
   d. packaging

8a. goes in one ear and out the other
   b. climb in and out of ears of corn
   c. doesn't pay attention (ears meaning parts of the body, not ears of corn)
   d. cornfield

9a. You are what you eat. (proverb)
   b. You become the food you eat.
   c. If you eat healthy foods, you'll be a healthy person in body and mind; if you eat junk, you'll be unhealthy.
   d. a guide to good nutrition, and the woman looks like a strawberry

10a. made for each other
   b. two "people" who were manufactured so they could be together
   c. two people who are perfectly suited for each other
   d. The person talking is standing near equipment found in a laboratory, and the people sitting on the sofa look like Dr. Frankenstein's creations.

IDIOMS III

1a. ran out of juice
   b. the orange had no more liquid inside
   c. ran out of energy
   d. stop in the middle

2a. sitting on top of the world
   b. A bride is sitting on top of a globe that represents the world.
   c. feeling wonderful, very happy
   d. The bride looks very happy.

3a. got a charge out of it
   b. enjoyed using it
   c. defer payment of a purchase
   d. credit card

4a. blow your own horn
   b. Buy a horn so you can play one you own.
   c. to boast or praise oneself
   d. The store sells musical instruments.

CHAPTER 5
ANSWER KEY

5a. Don't put all your eggs in one basket (proverb).
b. Don't place all your efforts or hopes in a single venture.
c. Eggs, which are breakable, are all piled in one basket, and the girl is likely to trip over the rock in her path and ruin the basket's contents.

6a. pay an arm and a leg
b. pay with body parts
c. pay a very high price
d. low, low prices

7a. animal magnetism
b. The large animal is like a magnet, which exerts a physical force to draw an object to itself.
c. an inner force some individuals have that can strongly influence others to react favorably to them
d. The large animal is attractive and appealing, so other animals may like it. The smaller animal is being pulled toward the larger one.

8a. has more holes than the other cheeses
b. acting as if you're better than others
c. The cheese with the most holes looks very proud, as if it is better than the other cheeses.

9a. the little woman
b. a woman small in size
c. a man's wife
d. The woman is very small.
e. It makes it seem as if a wife is less of a person than her husband.

10a. editor-in-chief
b. The editor will be eaten by and end up inside of the chief.
c. the chief editor of a newspaper
d. cannibal, because cannibals eat people

IDIOMS IV

1a. facing a hard decision; in a difficult position and not knowing what to do
b. very attentive, very eager to hear (amusing because Mr. Spock has large ears)
c. start from the beginning
d. put forth your best effort
e. to observe the ship's maximum operating force or power

2a. look out for number one
b. take care of yourself
c. that number one is the name of a particular individual
d. They are carrying weapons, so they can take care of themselves.

CHAPTER 5
ANSWER KEY

3a. leave all my children
 b. She can't leave her own offspring.
 c. She can't stop watching a television soap opera.
 d. The television announcer is saying, "And now back to 'All My Children.'"

4a. nobody's fool
 b. Frank, who is dressed as a fool (jester), doesn't belong to any of the people standing around him.
 c. a sensible and wise person who is not easily deceived
 d. Frank looks lost, as if he is waiting for someone to claim him.

5a. not playing with a full deck
 b. She's not using all the cards in the deck.
 c. She is mentally challenged.
 d. He doesn't have both oars in the water.
 e. He's rowing with one oar.
 f. He is mentally challenged.
 g. Two individuals who are alike are out together "in the same boat."

6a. soup to nuts
 b. They offer a complete menu, starting with soup and ending with dessert.
 c. They serve soup to eccentric or insane customers.
 d. identifying the clientele

7a. tasteless
 b. no flavor
 c. not showing good taste or manners, dull, uninteresting
 d. still chewing on it
 e. still chewing the pages with his teeth
 f. still thinking it over before forming an opinion
 g. hard to swallow
 h. difficult to get the pages down his throat to his stomach
 i. difficult to believe or to accept
 j. not showing good taste, still thinking it over before forming an opinion, and difficult to believe or accept, because they sound like comments made when reviewing a book

8a. quick as a bunny
 b. slow as a turtle
 c. The time on the rabbit clock is faster than the other clocks, and the time on the turtle clock is slower.

MATCHING INDIVIDUALS WITH THE APPROPRIATE "COMPLIMENTS"

1. C having good common sense, practical; Frankenstein has a flat (or level) head

2. D showing good sense, practical; ET is from another planet and came down to earth

CHAPTER 5 ANSWER KEY

3. E to act fairly, honestly; Wyatt Earp was a famous lawman who was an expert shot

4. A makes no errors, has no failures; a tennis player's error (such as hitting the ball beyond a specified line) is called a fault

5. B nicely dressed, presents a nice appearance; a man married five times has been a groom over and over again

IDIOMS AND PROVERBS FROM OTHER COUNTRIES

1. G
2. I
3. D
4. E
5. J
6. H
7. B
8. A
9. F
10. C

IDIOMS THAT MEAN THE SAME THING

1. quit working and go home
2. regard someone with scorn, contempt, or displeasure; think someone is not important
3. in all directions, in confusion
4. pause or hesitate while speaking, avoid giving a clear answer
5. become very angry, lose one's temper
6. quit, stop trying, surrender
7. become deeply interested and forget yourself while in deep thought or concentration
8. desert, leave alone in trouble, refuse to help or support
9. off the subject, about something different, not important to the subject being discussed
10. a soft, easy life; a pleasant or rich way of living
11. a very long time
12. be careful, thorough; pay close attention to details; do not make mistakes

IDIOMS AND PROVERBS WITH OPPOSITE MEANINGS

1. case that is simple, straightforward, without complication, easy to prove; without good proof or excuse, without good evidence or defense to offer

CHAPTER 5 ANSWER KEY

2. someone or something is exactly as appearances would lead you to believe; someone or something may or may not be exactly as appearances would lead you to believe

3. if many people work together, even a difficult job becomes easier; too many people trying to manage something simply spoil it

4. do not spend a penny more than necessary, be very thrifty; used to explain the loss of something that requires only a small amount of effort to get in the first place, and to describe the act of spending freely

5. defend successfully; stop fighting or arguing and do as the other side or other person wants, stop opposing

6. don't even think about it, may it never come true; keep something in the center of one's thoughts, give close attention

7. to deceive another; to be open and honest

8. to keep one's courage or spirits up, remain calm; to break into pieces (figuratively), to have an emotional breakdown

9. to fail to reach (some aim), to not succeed; to be equal, to be of high quality

10. (proverb) someone who is away for an extended period of time is remembered with increasing affection; (proverb) if one doesn't see someone or something for an extended period of time, one tends to forget about him/her or it

11. (proverb) make a decision quickly and then act upon it; (proverb) don't act impulsively, think carefully before acting

12. (proverb) used to describe how two people feel when they desire privacy and a third person is present; the more people who join in the fun, the better it will be

IDIOMS WITH ONLY A FIGURATIVE MEANING

1. being serious for a moment, in all seriousness
2. heavily armed with deadly weapons
3. to escape conviction and punishment
4. a letter or note to follow up on a visit, a thank-you note
5. just barely, by a narrow margin, with no room to spare
6. develop the feeling of love (for someone)
7. suddenly, spontaneously
8. to give or hold a party (for someone)

CHAPTER 5 ANSWER KEY

9. born with many advantages, born to a wealthy family
10. to contract a cold (the illness)
11. to be of little or no value
12. to travel fast, to make progress rapidly

FIXED-ORDER IDIOMS

1. L
2. D
3. J
4. A
5. E
6. F
7. I
8. B
9. G
10. C
11. H
12. K

MORE FIXED-ORDER IDIOMS

1. B
2. D
3. G
4. A
5. C
6. I
7. E
8. F
9. H

10a. No matter which way they go, they will have difficulty.
   b. about the same, one way or the other
   c. Hagar and his companion are in the same trouble no matter which direction they take, because equal numbers of the enemy are on both sides.

IDIOMS AND PHRASES WITH THREE WORDS IN FIXED ORDER

1. K
2. H
3. F
4. I
5. M
6. D
7. C
8. B
9. A
10. G
11. E
12. J
13. L

FIXED-ORDER IDIOM DEFINITIONS I, II, III, IV, V

No definitions are provided in this answer key for these fixed-order idioms. Please rely on your idiom dictionary.

CHAPTER 5 ANSWER KEY

MULTIPLE MEANING PHRASE DRAWINGS

Examples:

- he's beside himself; excited, disturbed, emotionally uncontrolled

- run down; to crash against and knock down or sink, to say bad things about, to criticize, to stop working, to not run or go, to get into poor condition, to look bad

MULTIPLE MEANING PHRASE DRAWINGS I

1. just between you and me; keep this secret, don't tell anyone else
2. right under your nose; in plain sight, right in front of you
3. square meal; well-balanced, full, nourishing, hearty meal
4. six feet underground; dead
5. read between the lines; to understand all of a writer's meaning by guessing at what was left unsaid
6. keep in touch; to remain in friendly communication with someone
7. go on forever; never stop
8. fill her up; to fill entirely, usually said by the driver of a car to a gas station attendant
9. six of one and a half dozen of the other; about the same one way or another, not a real choice, no difference
10. give up; to stop trying, surrender, yield
11. big deal; an unimportant, unimpressive thing or matter
12. water under the bridge; something that happened in the past and cannot be changed

MULTIPLE MEANING PHRASE DRAWINGS II

1. give her a big hand; loud and enthusiastic applause
2. go overboard; to do too much, to be extravagant
3. sitting on the fence; not able or not wanting to choose, undecided, in doubt
4. you can't have it both ways; you have to choose one way or the other
5. fed up; having had too much of something, at the end of one's patience, disgusted, bored
6. pain in the neck; an obnoxious or bothersome person

CHAPTER 5
ANSWER KEY

7. once upon a time; once, long ago, used to begin fairy tales
8. in over my head; having more difficulties than one can manage
9. drop in sometime; make a short or unplanned visit
10. cover up; to hide something wrong or bad from attention
11. down on his luck; having bad luck, having much trouble
12. dressed to kill; dressed in fancy or stylish clothes

"I'm a marvelous housekeeper. Every time I leave a man I keep his house."

Zsa Zsa Gabor

AMBIGUITY CAUSED BY CHANGES IN STRESS AND/OR JUNCTURE

CHAPTER GOALS

To enhance an individual's awareness of the role played by stress in determining sentence meaning

To improve an individual's understanding and use of ambiguities caused by changes in stress and/or juncture

TYPES OF ACTIVITIES PROVIDED

The activities in this chapter allow individuals to examine utterances in which ambiguity is caused by changes in stress and/or juncture in the following ways:

- using stress changes to determine sentence meaning; and
- determining the new meanings caused by stress and/or juncture changes in jokes, riddles, and cartoons.

BACKGROUND INFORMATION

- Understanding the ambiguities caused by changes in stress and/or juncture can be difficult because it requires the coordination of several metalinguistic skills. Word boundaries must be determined, the syllables of a word or a series of words have to be segmented and regrouped, and, in addition, some sound changes may be needed. All this needs to be done without the support of underlying meaning (Spector, 1990).

- Hirsch-Pasek, Gleitman, and Gleitman (1978) stated that riddles involving the aspects of language most concerned with meaning are easier to grasp than those involving surface properties such as stress and/or juncture. This can be shown by the ability of children to segment a sentence into words much earlier than they can segment words into syllables (Kamhi, Lee, and Nelson, 1985).

- Sometimes it is necessary to redefine words by combining rather than segmenting them. Consider the following riddle: "What would you do if you were starving on a desert island?" "Eat the sand which is there." Changing *sand which is* to *sandwiches* requires the elimination of two word boundaries and resequencing of the entire string of words to create a new meaning. The ability to recognize semantic clues in this riddle, such as *starving* and *eat*, is yet another necessary metalinguistic skill.

- "Knock-knock" jokes frequently are based on word-boundary manipulation. Consider this example: "Knock-knock." "Who's there?" "Amaryllis." "Amaryllis who?" "Amaryllis tate agent. Want to buy a house?" The word *Amaryllis* has to be segmented into *I'm a real es(tate)* for a person to discern the appropriate interpretation.

- When presenting an item orally, the placement of vocal stress will affect understanding a stress and/or juncture ambiguity. In the following riddle, the word *selfish* can be stressed differently to support a particular interpretation: "Why aren't fishermen generous?" "Their business makes them *sel*fish (or sell *fish*)."

- The manner of visual presentation also will affect an individual's understanding of stress and/or juncture items. Consider this example: "What songs do car radios play?" "Cartoons." If the printed response is presented as *Car tunes*, the individual may have less difficulty finding the ambiguous humor element. Or, changing the visual segmentation of the following stress/juncture-based knock-knock joke would be likely to affect comprehension: "Knock-knock." "Who's there?" "Justin." "Justin who?" "Justin (Just in) time for lunch."

USING STRESS TO DETERMINE SENTENCE MEANING

DIRECTIONS

For each of the following items, two questions will be asked. Underline the word or words in the answer sentence that would be stressed to make it an appropriate response to each of the questions. Say each sentence aloud, stressing the word or words you chose to underline. Use appropriate pauses. In the examples below, the highlighted (bold-faced) word or words would be underlined.

- Jack loves Grace.

    Who does Jack love? *Jack loves **Grace**.*

    Who loves Grace? ***Jack** loves Grace.*

- David sells really big chocolate chip cookies.

    What does David sell? *David sells really big **chocolate chip cookies**.*

    What size cookies does David sell? *David sells **really big** chocolate chip cookies.*

1. Kate caught a cold.

    a. What did Kate catch? *Kate caught a cold.*

    b. Who caught a cold? *Kate caught a cold.*

2. Rosalind drew a portrait of Gene.

    a. What did Rosalind do? *Rosalind drew a portrait of Gene.*

    b. Who drew a portrait? *Rosalind drew a portrait of Gene.*

3. Joanne read her baby books.

    a. What kind of books did Joanne read? *Joanne read her baby books.*

    b. To whom did Joanne read? *Joanne read her baby books.*

4. Liz loves lemon lollipops.

    a. What does Liz love? *Liz loves lemon lollipops.*

    b. What flavor lollipops does Liz love? *Liz loves lemon lollipops.*

5. Tarzan went swimming with Jane.

    a. What did Tarzan do with Jane? *Tarzan went swimming with Jane.*

    b. With whom did Tarzan swim? *Tarzan went swimming with Jane.*

USING STRESS TO DETERMINE SENTENCE MEANING

6. Gluttons gorge on gooey desserts.

    a. What do gluttons do? *Gluttons gorge on gooey desserts.*

    b. What kind of desserts do gluttons gorge on? *Gluttons gorge on gooey desserts.*

7. Bruce built a hummingbird house.

    a. What did Bruce build? *Bruce built a hummingbird house.*

    b. Who built a hummingbird house? *Bruce built a hummingbird house.*

8. On Monday, Mandy melted marshmallows.

    a. What did Mandy do? *On Monday, Mandy melted marshmallows.*

    b. When did Mandy melt marshmallows? *On Monday, Mandy melted marshmallows.*

9. Helen baked a cherry cheesecake.

    a. What did Helen bake? *Helen baked a cherry cheesecake.*

    b. What kind of cheesecake did Helen bake? *Helen baked a cherry cheesecake.*

10. The lighthouse keeper fell asleep.

    a. What did the lighthouse keeper do? *The lighthouse keeper fell asleep.*

    b. Who fell asleep? *The lighthouse keeper fell asleep.*

11. April rains bring beautiful flowers.

    a. What brings beautiful flowers? *April rains bring beautiful flowers.*

    b. What kind of flowers do April rains bring? *April rains bring beautiful flowers.*

12. Lee bought a purple polka-dot bikini.

    a. Who bought a bikini? *Lee bought a purple polka-dot bikini.*

    b. What kind of bikini did Lee buy? *Lee bought a purple polka-dot bikini.*

STRESS AND/OR JUNCTURE

DID YOU KNOW...

There are many instances when the meaning of a sentence changes when words, or parts of words, are stressed and joined together differently. For example, "What would you have if everyone in the country drove a pink Cadillac?" "A pink carnation." If the word *carnation* is separated, you have a nation full of pink cars. However, if you don't pause between *car* and *nation*, you have a pink flower.

DIRECTIONS

In the following examples, figure out which word or words give the new meaning if different stress is used when you say the sentence. For some of the items, spelling changes will occur. Complete the example items with someone. Then figure out the meanings of the words on the activity pages that follow. Answer the questions that follow each item.

- Q. What does an acorn say when it grows up?
  A. "Geometry!"

  a. Say the answer aloud very slowly. What does it sound like?

  _____

  b. What does the word in the answer mean? _____

  _____

  c. What does it become when the stress is changed? _____

  _____

  d. How was the new meaning caused? _____

  _____

  e. Which words in the question give you clues? _____

  _____

- Q. Whose name is mentioned in "The Star Spangled Banner"?
  A. José Canusi

  a. Say the answer aloud very slowly. Which words can be formed by separating the syllables of the words in the answer?

  _____

  b. Which words in the question give you a clue? _____

  _____

Chapter 6

STRESS AND/OR JUNCTURE I

1. Boy: "What are those holes in the lumber?"
   Carpenter: "Those are knotholes."
   Boy: "Well, they sure look like holes to me."

   a. Which word in the carpenter's answer was changed by separating the syllables? _____

   b. What did the carpenter mean? _____

   c. What did the boy think he meant? _____

2. Q. What kind of monk eats potato chips?
   A. A chipmunk.

   a. Which words are formed by separating a word in the answer? _____

   b. Which words in the question give you clues? _____

3. Q. Can you telephone from a spaceship?
   A. Of course. Who can't tell a phone from a spaceship?

   a. Which word in the question was changed by separating the syllables? _____

   b. What does the word mean in the question? _____

   c. What does it mean in the answer? _____

Q: WHAT COULD YOU DO IF YOU WERE STARVING ON A DESERT ISLAND?
A: EAT THE SAND WHICH IS THERE.

4. Look at the cartoon.

   a. Which words in the answer can be combined to form a new word? _____

   b. What do these words become? _____

   c. Which words in the riddle give you a clue? _____

   d. What do you see in the cartoon that gives you a clue? _____

Saying One Thing, Meaning Another © 1997 CC Spector. Published by Super Duper® Publications. Duplication permitted for educational use only.

STRESS AND/OR JUNCTURE I

5. Q. Why does it take a baseball player so long to run from second to third base?
   A. Because there's a short stop in between.

   a. Which words in the answer can be combined to form a new word?
   _____

   b. What is the new word and what does it mean? _____
   _____

   c. Which words in the question give you a clue? _____
   _____

6. Q. Who can always be found in the saddle?
   A. Rhoda Horse.

   a. Which word in the answer can be changed by separating the syllables?
   _____

   b. What does the word become? _____

   c. Why is this a good answer to the question? _____
   _____

7. Select the word that should be stressed for each picture.

   a. He fed her dog biscuits.   b. He fed her dog biscuits.

8. Q. Who never uses butter on her toast?
   A. Marge Orrin.

   a. What does the answer become when the words are combined?
   _____

   b. Which word in the question makes you think of the new answer?
   _____

207 | Chapter 6

STRESS AND/OR JUNCTURE I

9. That new book *How to Lose Weight* was written by X.R. Sizemore.

   a. What does the "author's" name really mean? _____

   b. Which words give you a clue? _____

10. Look at the cartoon.

    a. Which word was changed by separating the syllables?
    _____

    b. What does the word become? _____
    _____

    c. Does the cartoon give you any clues? _____
    _____
    _____
    _____
    _____

TEACHER: "CAN YOU USE THE WORD 'BUOYANT' IN A SENTENCE?"

ANDY: "YES, MA'AM. THE GIRL ANT WAS IN LOVE WITH THE BOY ANT."

11. Have you read the bestseller *Peekaboo* by I.C. Hugh?

    a. What does the "author's" name really mean? _____

    b. Where have you heard this before? _____
    _____

12. Q. Who wrote *The Earring Lover?*
    A. Pierce Steers.

    a. What does the answer become when the pause between the words and the stress are changed? _____

    b. Why are the new words a good answer to the question? _____
    _____
    _____

STRESS AND/OR JUNCTURE I

13. Knock-knock.
    Who's there?
    P.S.
    P.S. who? I thought your name was Adeline.
    Well, P.S. is when you Adeline.

    a. Which word can be changed by separating the syllables? _____

    b. What does it become? _____

    c. What clue can be found in this joke? _____

14. Q. Why did uncle put his wife in the freezer?
    A. He wanted to make auntie freeze.

    a. Which new word can be formed by combining two words in the answer? _____

    b. What does this new word mean? _____

    c. Which words in the question give you a clue for the original meaning? _____

15. Teacher: "Kathy, please use the word information in a sentence."
    Kathy: "Yes ma'am. During the air show, the Blue Angels flew in formation."

    a. Which word in the teacher's request was changed by separating the syllables? _____

    b. What does the word mean? _____

    c. What did it become in Kathy's answer? _____

    d. What is the new meaning? _____

16. Young child pointing to pool at a country club: "Why can't we swim at that pool?"
    Mom: "Because you have to belong."
    Child: "How long do you have to be?"

    a. Which word in Mom's response is the child using as two separate words? _____

    b. What does Mom mean by the word? _____

    c. What does the child take it to mean? _____

209 | Chapter 6

STRESS AND/OR JUNCTURE II

1. Q. Who wrote *The Great Diamond Robbery?*
   A. Jules Argon.

   a. Which words can be formed by separating the syllables of the last word in the answer? _____

   b. Why is this a good answer to the question? _____
   _____

2. Q. Who was Porky Pig's sharper cousin?
   A. Porky Pine.

   a. Which word can be formed by combining the words in the answer?
   _____

   b. Why is this a good answer to the question? _____
   _____

Q. IF A LITTLE CHICKEN COULD SPEAK AND FOUND AN ORANGE IN ITS NEST, WHAT DO YOU THINK IT WOULD SAY?

A. "OH, LOOK AT THE ORANGE MAMA LAID."

3. Look at the cartoon.

   a. What new word can be formed by combining the last two words in the answer? _____
   _____
   _____

   b. What does the new word mean? _____
   _____
   _____

4. Teacher: "Mark, please use the word despise in a sentence."
   Mark: "Yes ma'am. Yesterday de spies broke de secret code."

   a. What does the word *despise* mean in the question? _____
   _____

   b. What does it become in the answer? _____
   _____

STRESS AND/OR JUNCTURE II

5. Q. What did the computer say when the spaceship landed on Mars instead of Venus?
   A. I didn't planet that way.

   a. Which word in the answer will have a different meaning if the syllables are separated? _____

   b. What does it become? _____

   c. Why was the original word used? _____
   _____

6. A redheaded Russian named Rudolf looked out of the window one morning and said, "It's raining." His wife looked out and said, "No, it's sleeting." "No, no, it's raining," her husband said. "Rudolf the Red knows rain, dear!"

   a. Which words in the last part of the joke can be put together to sound like a song title? _____
   _____

   b. What does it become? _____
   _____

7. Q. Why aren't fishermen generous?
   A. Their business makes them selfish.

   a. Which word in the answer will have a different meaning if the syllables are separated? _____

   b. What does it become? _____

   c. Which word in the question gives you a clue? _____
   _____

8. Q. What is the life story of a car called?
   A. An autobiography.

   a. Which word in the answer will have a different meaning if the syllables are separated? _____

   b. What does it become? _____

   c. Which words in the question give you clues? _____
   _____

211 | Chapter 6

© 1997 CC Spector. Published by Super Duper® Publications.
Duplication permitted for educational use only.

STRESS AND/OR JUNCTURE II

9. Joe replaced a bulb at the top of the Empire State Building. He said it was the highlight of his career.

   a. Which word in this joke will have a different meaning if the syllables are separated? _____

   b. What does it become? _____

   c. Which words in the joke give you a clue? _____
   _____

10. Two weevils started life together. One was an immediate success, the other a complete failure. Naturally, the latter became known as the lesser of two weevils.

    a. Which two words can be stressed differently to change their meaning?
    _____

    b. What do they be come? _____

    c. What does the phrase mean with the new stress? _____
    _____

11. Teacher: "Harry, can you use the word centimeter in a sentence?
    Harry: "Sure. My sister was walking home from school, so I was sent to meet her."

    a. What does the word centimeter mean in the question? _____
    _____

    b. How did Harry change the word *centimeter* by separating the syllables?
    _____

12. Look at the want ad.

    Wanted
    Manager for
    large resort hotel.
    Must be inn experienced.

    a. Which words can be combined to form a new word? _____
    _____

    b. What do these words mean in the want ad? _____
    _____

    c. What is the new word? _____

    d. What does the new word mean? _____

STRESS AND/OR JUNCTURE II

13. Look at the cartoon.

    Q. WHICH VEGETABLE HAS CONVERSATIONS WITH JACK?

    A. JACK AND THE BEANS TALK.

    a. Which words in the answer can have another meaning? _____

    b. What do they become if you combine them and change the stress? _____
    _____

    c. Does the cartoon give you any clues? _____
    _____
    _____

14. "Did you hear about the award-winning farmer? He was outstanding in his field."

    a. Which word in the answer can be changed by separating the syllables?
    _____

    b. What does it become? _____

    c. What does the original word mean in the answer? _____
    _____

    d. What does it mean with the syllables separated? _____
    _____

    e. Which words in the question give you a clue for the original meaning?
    _____

15. Don: "My wife is taking a trip to the West Indies."
    Juan: "Jamaica?"
    Don: "Not at all. She wanted to go."

    a. What did Juan mean when he said Jamaica? _____
    _____

    b. What did Don take Jamaica to mean? _____

    c. What gives you a clue for Don's interpretation? _____
    _____

STRESS AND/OR JUNCTURE II

16.

A ROUND TUIT

THIS IS A TUIT.
TAKE GOOD CARE OF IT AS TUITS ARE
HARD TO COME BY, ESPECIALLY THE
ROUND ONES. THIS IS AN INDISPENSABLE ITEM.
IT WILL HELP YOU BECOME A MORE EFFICIENT
WORKER. FOR YEARS WE HAVE HEARD PEOPLE
SAY, "I'LL DO IT WHEN I GET A ROUND TUIT."
NOW THAT YOU HAVE ONE,
YOU CAN ACCOMPLISH ALL THOSE
THINGS YOU SAID YOU WOULD.

a. Which words on this sign can be combined differently to change their meaning? _____

b. What do the words become? _____

c. Which words give you a clue for the newly formed meaning?
_____

Saying One Thing, Meaning Another

BOOKS YOU WON'T FIND AT THE LIBRARY

DIRECTIONS

The following jokes are based on changes in stress and the way the words are joined together to form the "authors'" names. Use the "book" title to determine what each "author's" name really means. Say the name aloud, slowly.

Example:

- *Monster Making as a Hobby* by Frank N. Stine. The word *monster* in the "book" title helps you see that the "author's" name becomes *Frankenstein*.

1. *Put Kids to Work* by Hiram Young

   The "author's" name means _____

2. *The Tiresome Talker* by Boris Stiff

   The "author's" name means _____

3. *Demolition Derby* by Rex Carrs

   The "author's" name means _____

4. *A New Slant on Life* by Eileen Sideways

   The "author's" name means _____

5. *Raindrops Keep Fallin' on My Head* by Rufus Leakin

   The "author's" name means _____

6. *Smalltime Thief* by Robin A. Piggybank

   The "author's" name means _____

7. *The Heavy Burden* by Aiken Back

   The "author's" name means _____

8. *Saddle Sores* by Rhoda Bronco

   The "author's" name means _____

9. *Heaven Forbid* by Shirley Knott

   The "author's" name means _____

10. *This Is the End* by Saul Over

    The "author's" name means _____

BOOKS YOU WON'T FIND AT THE LIBRARY

11. *How to Get Rich Quick* by Meg A. Bucks
    The "author's" name means _____

12. *Uncovering Magic Tricks* by Howie Diddit
    The "author's" name means _____

13. *How to Be Unique* by Freida B. Mee
    The "author's" name means _____

14. *The Great Pyramids* by Fay Roe
    The "author's" name means _____

15. *The Empty Tank* by Phil R. Upp
    The "author's" name means _____

16. *Who Makes the Best Pies?* by Howard I. Know
    The "author's" name means _____

17. *Why You Need Insurance* by Justin Case
    The "author's" name means _____

18. *The Woman Who Fell Out of the Window* by Eileen Dover
    The "author's" name means _____

19. *Guide to Justice* by Dolores Cleer
    The "author's" name means _____

20. *Is It Really Love?* by Midas Welby
    The "author's" name means _____

21. *A Guide to Understanding Werewolves* by Justin Casey Howells
    The "author's" name means _____

22. *Primitive Warfare* by Beau N. Arros
    The "author's" name means _____

23. *Mixing Dangerous Chemicals* by Yul B. Sari
    The "author's" name means

24. *My Life at the North Pole* by I.M. Freezen
    The "author's" name means _____

"KNOCK-KNOCK" JOKES

DIRECTIONS

"Knock-knock" jokes frequently are based on changes in stress and the way the words are joined together. To practice these changes, try this sample "knock-knock":

- Knock-knock.
  Who's there?
  Thatcher.
  Thatcher who?
  Thatcher idea of a joke?

  a. Which word can be stressed differently to change its meaning?
  _____

  b. What does it become? _____

1. Knock-knock.
   Who's there?
   Sawyer.
   Sawyer who?
   Sawyer picture in the paper.

   a. Which word can be stressed differently to change its meaning?
   _____

   b. What does it become? _____

2. Knock-knock.
   Who's there?
   Mikey.
   Mikey who?
   Mikey will open this door.

   a. Which word can be stressed differently to change its meaning?
   _____

   b. What does it become? _____

3. Knock-knock.
   Who's there?
   Arthur.
   Arthur who?
   Arthur mometer says it's hot today.

   a. Which words can be stressed differently to change their meaning?
   _____

   b. What does it become? _____

Chapter 6

"KNOCK-KNOCK" JOKES

4. Knock-knock.
   Who's there?
   Pasture.
   Pasture who?
   Pasture bedtime, isn't it?

   a. Which word can be stressed differently to change its meaning?
   _____

   b. What does it become? _____

5. Knock-knock.
   Who's there?
   Henrietta.
   Henrietta who?
   Henrietta grasshopper.

   a. Which word can be stressed differently to change its meaning?
   _____

   b. What does it become? _____

   c. Does the cartoon give you a clue? _____

6. Knock-knock.
   Who's there?
   Dewey.
   Dewey who?
   Dewey have to keep telling knock-knock jokes?

   a. Which word can be stressed differently to change its meaning?
   _____

   b. What does it become? _____

"KNOCK-KNOCK" JOKES

7. Knock-knock.

   Who's there?

   Anita.

   Anita who?

   Anita good punch line for this joke.

   a. Which word can be stressed differently to change its meaning?

   _____

   b. What does it become? _____

8. Knock-knock.

   Who's there?

   Seymour.

   Seymour who?

   Seymour if you would open the door.

   a. Which word can be stressed differently to change its meaning?

   _____

   b. What does it become? _____

9. Knock-knock.

   Who's there?

   Tennis.

   Tennis who?

   Tennis five plus five.

   a. Which word can be stressed differently to change its meaning?

   _____

   b. What does it become? _____

10. Knock-knock.

    Who's there?

    Lena.

    Lena who?

    Lena little closer and I'll tell you.

    a. Which word can be stressed differently to change its meaning?

    _____

    b. What does it become? _____

CREATING "KNOCK-KNOCK" JOKES

DIRECTIONS

Make your own "knock-knock" jokes using the following words. The format has been set up for you. Fill in the punch line. Think about how each word could be broken down into other words, then use those words to begin your punch line.

1. *ammonia*
   Knock-knock.
   Who's there?
   Ammonia.
   Ammonia who?

   _____
   _____

2. *pencil*
   Knock-knock.
   Who's there?
   Pencil.
   Pencil who?

   _____
   _____

3. *lettuce*
   Knock-knock.
   Who's there?
   Lettuce.
   Lettuce who?

   _____
   _____

4. *unaware*
   Knock-knock.
   Who's there?
   Unaware.
   Unaware who?

   _____
   _____

CREATING "KNOCK-KNOCK" JOKES

5. *cellar*
   Knock-knock.
   Who's there?
   Cellar.
   Cellar who?

   _____
   _____

6. *letter*
   Knock-knock.
   Who's there?
   Letter.
   Letter who?

   _____
   _____

7. *rabbit*
   Knock-knock.
   Who's there?
   Rabbit.
   Rabbit who?

   _____
   _____

8. *handsome*
   Knock-knock.
   Who's there?
   Handsome.
   Handsome who?

   _____
   _____

9. *butter*
   Knock-knock.
   Who's there?
   Butter.
   Butter who?

   _____
   _____

CREATING "KNOCK-KNOCK" JOKES

10. *Justin*
    Knock-knock.
    Who's there?
    Justin.
    Justin who?

    _____

    _____

11. *Betty*
    Knock-knock.
    Who's there?
    Betty.
    Betty who?

    _____

    _____

12. *Europe*
    Knock-knock.
    Who's there?
    Europe.
    Europe who?

    _____

    _____

ADDITIONAL ACTIVITIES

1. Ask individuals to make up more names of "authors," such as those found in the "Books You Won't Find at the Library" activity. The title of the "book" should bear some relationship to the "author's" name.

2. Encourage individuals to create or collect "knock-knock" jokes. Discuss how the changes in stress and/or juncture create new meanings.

3. Suggest that the individuals look through the dictionary to find words (or provide words) that have a different meaning when the stress is changed (for example, *minute,* as in "Just a minute" or "That is a minute amount of ice cream"). Discuss the two meanings of each word.

CHAPTER 6 ANSWER KEY

These answers are merely guidelines. The facilitator can judge if the individual's responses are appropriate for each item.

USING STRESS TO DETERMINE SENTENCE MEANING

1a. a cold
 b. Kate

2a. drew a portrait
 b. Rosalind

3a. baby books
 b. her baby

4a. lemon lollipops
 b. lemon

5a. went swimming
 b. Jane

6a. gorge (or gorge on gooey desserts)
 b. gooey

7a. a hummingbird house
 b. Bruce

8a. melted marshmallows
 b. On Monday

9a. a cherry cheesecake
 b. cherry

10a. fell asleep
 b. The lighthouse keeper

11a. April rains
 b. beautiful

12a. Lee
 b. purple polka-dot

STRESS AND/OR JUNCTURE

Examples:

- a. ge om et ry = Gee, I'm a tree
  b. a branch of mathematics
  c. Gee, I'm a tree.
  d. The stress was changed from the second syllable to the first, and a pause was added.
  e. acorn, when it grows up

- a. Oh say can you see
  b. "The Star Spangled Banner," because these are the first words in this song, which is the national anthem of the United States

CHAPTER 6 ANSWER KEY

STRESS AND/OR JUNCTURE I

1a. knotholes
 b. a hole in a board where a knot has come out
 c. not holes

2a. chip monk
 b. monk, chips

3a. telephone
 b. make a phone call
 c. know the difference between a phone and a spaceship

4a. sand which is
 b. sandwiches
 c. starving, eat (because these words relate to food)
 d. sandwiches in the sand toward which a hungry man is crawling

5a. short stop
 b. shortstop, a position on a baseball team
 c. baseball player, second to third base

6a. Rhoda
 b. rode a
 c. because a saddle is used when riding a horse

7a. her
 b. dog

8a. margarine
 b. butter

9a. exercise more
 b. how to lose weight

10a. buoyant
 b. boy ant
 c. yes, one of the ants is a boy, and the log is floating (it is buoyant)

11a. I see you
 b. game played with babies

12a. pierced ears
 b. because the "book" title refers to earrings

13a. Adeline
 b. add a line
 c. P.S. (postscript), which means something added to a written message

14a. antifreeze
 b. a fluid used in vehicles to keep the engine from freezing in winter
 c. uncle, wife, freezer

CHAPTER 6 ANSWER KEY

15a. information
  b. knowledge
  c. in formation
  d. performing in a specific pattern or grouping

16a. belong
  b. to be a member of a club
  c. to be long, to be of a certain length

STRESS AND/OR JUNCTURE II

1a. jewels are gone
 b. because the "book" concerns a robbery about diamonds, which are jewels

2a. porcupine
 b. because a porcupine has quills with sharp points

3a. marmalade
 b. a kind of preserve or jam

4a. hate, regard with scorn
 b. de (the) spies

5a. planet
 b. plan it
 c. because Mars and Venus are planets

6a. Rudolf the Red knows rain, dear
 b. Rudolf the red-nosed reindeer

7a. selfish
 b. sell fish
 c. fishermen

8a. autobiography
 b. auto biography
 c. life story, car

9a. highlight
 b. high light
 c. Empire State Building, because it's one of the tallest buildings in New York

10a. two weevils
  b. two evils
  c. when two things are evil, the one that seems to be less evil than the other

11a. a unit of length in the metric system
  b. sent to meet her

CHAPTER 6
ANSWER KEY

12a. inn experienced
  b. knowledgeable about running an inn (hotel)
  c. inexperienced
  d. having no experience

13a. beans talk
  b. beanstalk
  c. yes, you can see a beanstalk

14a. outstanding
  b. out standing
  c. standing out from a group (excellence)
  d. standing while out in his field
  e. award-winning

15a. an island in the West Indies
  b. d'ya (did you) make her
  c. his response that she wanted to go

16a. a Round Tuit
  b. around to it
  c. I'll do it when I get a Round Tuit

BOOKS YOU WON'T FIND AT THE LIBRARY

1. hire 'em (them) young
2. bore us stiff
3. wrecks cars
4. I lean sideways
5. roof is leaking
6. robbing a piggybank
7. aching back
8. rode a bronco
9. surely not
10. (it)'s all over
11. megabucks
12. how he did it
13. free to be me
14. pharaoh
15. fill her up
16. how would I know
17. just in case
18. I leaned over
19. the law is clear
20. might as well be
21. just in case he howls
22. bow and arrows
23. you'll be sorry
24. I am freezing

CHAPTER 6 ANSWER KEY

"KNOCK-KNOCK" JOKES

Example:
- a. Thatcher
  b. (is) that your

1a. Sawyer
 b. saw your

2a. Mikey
 b. my key

3a. Arthur
 b. our ther(mometer)

4a. Pasture
 b. past your

5a. Henrietta
 b. Henry et(ate) a
 c. yes, he is thinking about a grasshopper and licking his lips

6a. Dewey
 b. do we

7a. Anita
 b. I need a

8a. Seymour
 b. see more

9a. Tennis
 b. ten is

10a. Lena
  b. lean a

CREATING "KNOCK-KNOCK" JOKES

(Note: These are example answers. Many other answers are acceptable.)

1. ammonia—I'm only a bird in a gilded cage.
2. pencil—Pants will fall down if you don't wear a belt.
3. lettuce—Let us go out for some ice cream.
4. unaware—Underwear is on sale today.
5. cellar—Sell her a soda and let's all go home.
6. letter—Let her come in, the door is not locked.
7. rabbit—Wrap it up and I'll take it.
8. handsome—Hand some of that pie over here.
9. butter—But her mother won't let you in.
10. Justin—Just in time for dinner.
11. Betty—Bet he won't eat your cooking.
12. Europe—You're up to no good.

7

Good enough never is.

CLARIFYING AMBIGUOUS UTTERANCES

CHAPTER GOALS

To improve an individual's skill in asking for and providing information that will clarify ambiguous utterances

To improve an individual's awareness of the needs of the listener in a conversation

TYPES OF AMBIGUITY

This chapter includes activities for understanding ambiguity caused by pragmatic and cognitive factors. The activities focus on the following types of ambiguous utterances:

- utterances with inadequate information (for example, "Meet me *there* next week");

- utterances with vague pronominal references (for example, "Jim said I should give it to *her*"); and

- utterances wrongly assuming world knowledge (regarding the speaker, the context, the purpose of the verbal interaction, and so on [for example, "You can't expect everyone to *feel the way you do about that*"]).

TYPES OF ACTIVITIES PROVIDED

This chapter provides the following activities:

- restating an ambiguous utterance with appropriate additional information; and

- determining the appropriate questions to ask when clarification of an utterance is necessary.

BACKGROUND INFORMATION

- Individuals with poor presuppositional skills often make faulty assumptions about the knowledge their listeners have about a topic being discussed. Unless listeners know what has been said (or done) before the comments were made, there will be information gaps that can affect their understanding of the topic under discussion.

- It is possible to improve an individual's awareness of what is missing in comments that cause them to be ambiguous to a listener (Larson and McKinley, 1987, 1995; Nippold, 1991).

- Some individuals do not know how to go about finding information that will clarify comments they find ambiguous. They have to be taught strategies for forming appropriate questions (Buttrill, Niizawa, Biemer, Takakashi, and Hearn, 1989; Schumaker, Deshler, Alley, and Warner, 1983; Seidenberg, 1988). They also have to be taught strategies for clarifying utterances they make by restating the utterances with the appropriate additional information.

- Learning is maximized when the individual is made aware of important features of the material considered (Seidenberg, 1988).

SUGGESTIONS FOR FACILITATORS

1. Discuss the examples in great detail so that individuals will understand how to restate each comment.

2. "Brainstorm" possible questions to ask that will lead to clarification of the ambiguous comment.

3. Use the "w's" (*who[m], what, where, why, which,* and *when,* plus *how*) as a checklist of questions to consider.

4. Take any ambiguous comments that arise in conversation and help individuals develop clarification questions and restatements.

5. Use the answer key at the end of this section as a guideline for possible responses.

RESTATING AMBIGUOUS COMMENTS

DID YOU KNOW...

There are times when we make comments and we assume our conversational partner knows what happened or what was said just before we made the comments. This is not always true. If, for example, you come into a room and your friend says, "Jim will be joining us for the movie this evening," your friend assumes that you know Jim and that you know about the plan to see a particular movie. All of these assumptions may be true, in which case there is no problem understanding the comment. However, if these are incorrect assumptions, then the comment becomes unclear, or ambiguous.

DIRECTIONS

The following items contain comments that depend on knowing who is speaking, what happened, or what was said before the comment was made. Suggestions are given to help you determine what you need to know to ensure that the comment will be clear and easy to understand. Restate the comment in each of the following items so that anyone would understand what it means. Use any appropriate details you desire. Be sure to check for clues by looking at who is making the comment, who is listening, and the type of comment being made. Complete the examples below with someone. Then do the items that follow on the next pages.

- Judy said to her friend Anna Marie: "I really enjoyed going to that new restaurant with him."

    I need to know: a. Which new restaurant Judy was talking about
    b. To whom Judy was referring when she said "him"

    Restate the comment so that it would be clear to anyone.
    For example: "I really enjoyed going to Salisbury, the new steak restaurant, with my boyfriend, John."

    Restate the comment a different way. _____

    _____

- Naomi said to her Dad: "If you give me money, I can buy it before they close."

    I need to know: a. What Naomi wants to buy
    b. What is going to close

    Restate the comment so that it would be clear to anyone.
    For example: "If you give me money for an ice cream cone, I can buy it before the soda fountain closes."

    Restate the comment a different way. _____

    _____

RESTATING AMBIGUOUS COMMENTS

1. Glady said to her friend Rose: "Last time I ate there, I ended up in the hospital."

    I need to know: a. Where Glady ate

    b. What happened that caused her to go to the hospital

    Restate the comment so that it would be clear to anyone.

    _____

    _____

2. A salesperson said to a customer: "If you buy both packages, we'll give you the two-for-one special."

    I need to know: a. What the customer is considering buying

    b. What is meant by "the two-for-one special"

    Restate the comment so that it would be clear to anyone.

    _____

    _____

3. Jessica said to Jeff: "That is so annoying. I wish he would stop, I can hardly hear."

    I need to know: a. To whom Jessica is referring

    b. What he is doing that annoys her

    c. What Jessica is trying to hear

    Restate the comment so that it would be clear to anyone.

    _____

    _____

4. Mother said to her daughter Mindy: "Must she leave those things in there?"

    I need to know: a. To whom Mother is referring

    b. What Mother means by "those things"

    c. What Mother means by "in there"

    Restate the comment so that it would be clear to anyone.

    _____

    _____

RESTATING AMBIGUOUS COMMENTS

5. Melissa said to Nicole: "You have to find my other one in that mess before I'll let you borrow this one."

   I need to know: a. What Melissa means by "this one"

   b. What Melissa is referring to as "my other one"

   c. What Melissa means by "that mess"

   Restate the comment so that it would be clear to anyone.

   _____
   _____

6. Dillon said to Daniel: "I hate when she talks to me that way."

   I need to know: a. To whom Dillon is referring

   b. How she spoke to Dillon

   Restate the comment so that it would be clear to anyone.

   _____
   _____

7. Danya said to Alec: "Try moving it over there."

   I need to know: a. What is being moved

   b. Where Danya means by "over there"

   Restate the comment so that it would be clear to anyone.

   _____
   _____

8. Jake said to Jill: "Hey, this was fun. Let's do it again next week. Same time, same place."

   I need to know: a. What Jake and Jill did that was fun

   b. When they did it

   c. Where they did it

   d. On what day next week Jake wants to do it again

   Restate the comment so that it would be clear to anyone.

   _____
   _____

RESTATING AMBIGUOUS COMMENTS

9. A teenage boy said: "If you buy it for me, I'll never ask for anything again."

   I need to know: a. To whom he is speaking
   b. What he wants the person to buy for him

   Restate the comment so that it would be clear to anyone.

   _____

   _____

10. Hannah said to Aaron: "She left them at school. Now I'll have to go back to pick them up."

    I need to know: a. To whom Hannah is referring
    b. What "she" left at school

    Restate the comment so that it would be clear to anyone.

    _____

    _____

11. The manager said to Whitney, a salesperson: "I'm glad you got here in time. Leave your list on my desk before you go to the meeting."

    I need to know: a. Why the manager was glad Whitney got there in time
    b. What list the manager is talking about
    c. What meeting the manager is talking about

    Restate the comment so that it would be clear to anyone.

    _____

    _____

12. Helene said to Bill: "Bert and Ernie died because the glass broke."

    I need to know: a. Who Bert and Ernie are
    b. What kind of glass breakage could cause Bert and Ernie to die

    Restate the comment so that it would be clear to anyone.

    _____

    _____

DETERMINING INFORMATION NEEDED TO CLARIFY AMBIGUITY

DIRECTIONS

In the following items, determine what information is needed to ensure that the comment will be clear and easy to understand. Keep in mind the basic types of questions you can ask to find out what you need to know. These are questions that start with *who(m), what, where, why, when, which,* or *how*. Restate the comment in each of the following items so that anyone could understand what it means. Use any appropriate details you desire. Be sure to check for clues by looking at who is making the comment, who is listening, and the type of comment being made. Complete the examples below with someone. Then complete the items on the next pages.

- One student said to another: "Do you think even she could have answered the third one?"

  I need to know: _____

  _____

  Restate the comment so that it would be clear to anyone. For example, "Do you think even Norma, the best math student in the class, could have answered the third question on the math test?"

  Restate the comment a different way: _____

  _____

  _____

- Marty said to Sandy: "I hope it will be dry soon. I can't start until it is."

  I need to know: _____

  _____

  Restate the comment so that it would be clear to anyone. For example, "I hope the kitchen floor will be dry soon. I can't start preparing dinner until it is."

  Restate the comment a different way: _____

  _____

  _____

DETERMINING INFORMATION NEEDED TO CLARIFY AMBIGUITY

1. Christine: "Please pass that over here."

    I need to know: a. _____

    b. _____

    c. _____

    Restate the comment so that it would be clear to anyone.

    _____
    _____

2. A male professor said to a student: "Be sure to send it over here before I leave."

    I need to know: a. _____

    b. _____

    c. _____

    Restate the comment so that it would be clear to anyone.

    _____
    _____

3. Alyse said to Richard: "I just loved that book. Next time you're at the library, get me another one by the same author."

    I need to know: a. _____

    b. _____

    Restate the comment so that it would be clear to anyone.

    _____
    _____

4. Shelby hissed at Max: "Get away from that before I claw you."

    I need to know: a. _____

    b. _____

    Restate the comment so that it would be clear to anyone.

    _____
    _____

DETERMINING INFORMATION NEEDED TO CLARIFY AMBIGUITY

5. Alfie said to Mandy: "Let's give him 10 more minutes before we start."

   I need to know: a. _____

   b. _____

   Restate the comment so that it would be clear to anyone.

   _____

   _____

6. Jerry said to Martha: "Let's take them along. It will be easier."

   I need to know: a. _____

   b. _____

   c. _____

   Restate the comment so that it would be clear to anyone.

   _____

   _____

7. Phyllis said to Bruce: "Next time you're in that neighborhood, don't forget to visit our favorite spot."

   I need to know: a. _____

   b. _____

   Restate the comment so that it would be clear to anyone.

   _____

   _____

8. Betty said to Jim: "Make it short this time, so we don't have to do it again so soon."

   I need to know: a. _____

   b. _____

   Restate the comment so that it would be clear to anyone.

   _____

   _____

DETERMINING INFORMATION NEEDED TO CLARIFY AMBIGUITY

9. Barbara said to Ken: "Don't forget to change the setting, or we'll end up being late."

   I need to know: a. _____

   b. _____

   c. _____

   Restate the comment so that it would be clear to anyone.

   _____

   _____

10. The chef said to his assistant: "Be sure to put it in a bowl that has plenty of ice around it before you put it out."

    I need to know: a. _____

    b. _____

    Restate the comment so that it would be clear to anyone.

    _____

    _____

ADDITIONAL ACTIVITIES

1. Have individuals analyze an ambiguous comment made to them by a friend, teacher, or parent. Try to figure out why the comment was made and what was meant by the comment.

2. Have individuals analyze characters they know from one or more TV series in which the characters have ongoing roles. Knowledge of a particular character can provide background knowledge and prior utterances on which to base an interpretation of an otherwise ambiguous comment.

3. Stress the need for individuals to listen carefully to the tone of the speaker's voice when a comment is made, as well as noting the speaker's facial expression, gestures, body language, and so forth. Practice by having different speakers say something in a prearranged manner (for example, teasingly, angrily, sarcastically, or lovingly), and have individuals determine the speakers' intentions.

4. Have individuals use a telephone or conduct room-to-room conversations in which the speaker and the listener cannot see each other. Then have the speaker describe something to the listener so that it is clear and easy to understand.

5. When using a telephone or room-to-room conversations, help listeners develop appropriate questions to ask that will clarify any ambiguities in the messages they hear.

6. Use barrier activities to help speakers and listeners improve their awareness of the needs of their conversational partners. Speakers can describe visual clues that may clarify ambiguities, and listeners can request appropriate information that will help them to understand the messages.

CHAPTER 7 ANSWER KEY

The restated comments provided for all of the answers that follow are just examples. Each individual's restatement will be unique.

RESTATING AMBIGUOUS COMMENTS

Examples: Answers will vary.

1. "Last time I ate chicken salad at Mabel's Diner, I got food poisoning and ended up in the hospital."

2. "If you buy two packages, each containing four cassette tapes, we'll give you the two-for-one-price special, which is $10."

3. "That man in front of me is coughing so much, I wish he would stop. I can hardly hear the movie."

4. "Must your friend Karen leave her ice skates in the living room?"

5. "Find my sweater in that mess on the floor of your room before I'll let you borrow another one of my sweaters."

6. "I hate when my mother talks to me as if I were a little baby."

7. "Try moving the new lamp next to the blue chair."

8. "Hey, riding our bikes on the mountain bike trail was fun. Let's do it again next week. See you Saturday at 10 a.m. at the entrance to the park."

9. "Mom, if you buy that used car for me, I'll never ask for anything again."

10. "Our daughter Ann left her glasses at school. Now I'll have to go back and pick them up."

11. "I'm glad you got here before the new vice president starts the meeting to decide which new products the store should offer. Leave your list of suggestions about the new products on my desk."

12. "My goldfish, Bert and Ernie, died when the glass of their fish tank broke and all the water flowed out."

DETERMINING INFORMATION NEEDED TO CLARIFY AMBIGUITY

Examples:

- To whom the student is referring
  What is meant by "the third one"

- What "it" refers to
  What Marty wants to start doing

   1a. to whom Christine is talking
    b. what she is referring to
    c. where she wants it passed
      "Doug, please pass the salt to this end of the table."

CHAPTER 7
ANSWER KEY

2a. what "it" refers to
 b. where he wants it sent
 c. when he is leaving
 "Please be sure to send your final report to my office before 5 o'clock."

3a. what the book is called
 b. the author's name
 "I just loved *The Good Earth*. Next time you're at the library, get me another book by Pearl S. Buck."

4a. who the "speaker" and listener are
 b. what "that" refers to
 "Max, you big dog, get away from my cat food before I claw you."

5a. who "him" refers to
 b. what Alfie and Mandy are planning to start
 "Let's give Uncle Stan 10 more minutes to get here before we starting eating our dinner."

6a. who "them" refers to
 b. where Jerry and Martha want to take them
 c. why it would be easier
 "Let's take the kids along with us to the mall. It will be easier than finding a baby-sitter."

7a. to which neighborhood Phyllis is referring
 b. what their favorite spot is
 "Next time you're in Palo Alto, don't forget to visit the Sculpture Garden."

8a. what "it" refers to
 b. what they would have to do again
 "Cut the grass shorter than you did last time, so we don't have to cut it again so soon."

9a. what "the setting" refers to
 b. why they would be late
 c. what they would be late for
 "Don't forget to change the setting on the clock now that it's daylight saving time, or we'll get up late for work in the morning."

10a. what the chef means by "it"
 b. where he wants his assistant to put it
 "Be sure to put the shrimp in a bowl with plenty of ice before you put it on the buffet table."

GLOSSARY

Ambiguous. Capable of being understood in two or more possible senses; doubtful, uncertain, obscure.

Brainstorming. A group problem-solving technique that involves the spontaneous contribution from all members of the group.

Figurative Language. Expressions that use words or phrases to represent an abstract concept; cannot be interpreted literally. Idioms, proverbs, metaphors, and similes are types of figurative language.

Homograph. A word that sounds the same and is spelled the same as another word but has a different meaning.

Homophone. A word that sounds the same as another word but has a different meaning and a different spelling.

Idiom. An expression unique to a language, especially one whose sense is not predictable from the meanings and arrangement of its elements (e.g., "Face the music").

Inferencing skills. Skills needed to derive a conclusion from facts or premises; guess, surmise, deduce, conclude.

Irony. Stating one meaning when the opposite meaning is intended (e.g., "I just love getting caught in heavy traffic").

Metacognition. The voluntary, selective attention to one's own cognitive processes, such as knowing about attending, organizing, remembering, inferencing, sequencing, and problem solving (van Kleeck, 1987).

Metalinguistic Awareness. The ability to reflect on language as an entity and the ability to analyze language into its linguistic components (van Kleeck, 1987).

Metaphor. A figure of speech in which a word or phrase literally denoting one kind of object or idea is used in place of another to suggest a likeness or analogy between them (e.g., "Her smile is pure sunshine").

Metapragmatic skills. Those skills necessary for the reception and communication of ideas. They involve one's conscious awareness of the cultural rules for using language efficiently in various social contexts (van Kleeck, 1987).

NONLINGUISTIC CUES. Coding devices that contribute to communication but are not a part of speech. These devices include gestures, body posture, facial expressions, head and body movements, eye contact, and distance between speaker and listener.

PARALINGUISTIC CUES. Use of the vocal tract to modify the utterances they affect (e.g., vocal intensity, speed, rhythm, intonation, and pitch).

PARAPHRASE. Restatement, giving the meaning in another form; the rewording of an expression or text as an explanation, clarification, or translation.

PRAGMATICS. Aspect of language concerning how the meaning conveyed by a word or sentence depends on aspects of context in which it is used (e.g., time, place, social relationship between speaker and listener, and speaker's assumptions about the listener's beliefs).

PRAGMATIC SKILLS. Skills needed to apply the cultural rules for using language efficiently in various social contexts (includes conversational skills).

PRESUPPOSITION. Supposing something in advance, with or without sufficient information.

PROVERB. A brief, popular adage or maxim used to teach a moral; figure of speech that generally gives advice (e.g., "Look before you leap").

REPAIR STRATEGIES. Ways in which miscommunications can be rendered clear and unambiguous (e.g., restatement in a louder voice, paraphrasing, using gestures or facial expressions, or providing necessary information previously left unstated).

SARCASM. Comments intended to be nasty, cutting, or contemptuous that state one meaning when the opposite meaning is intended (e.g., teacher to student who failed a test: "Well, you must have studied all night").

SIMILE. A figure of speech comparing two unlike things, often introduced by *like* or *as* (e.g., "She eats like a bird").

APPENDIX A

POPULATIONS WHO CAN BENEFIT FROM SAYING ONE THING, MEANING ANOTHER

NORMALLY ACHIEVING INDIVIDUALS

At one time or another, everyone has experienced confusion when trying to grasp the meaning of an ambiguous word or phrase. For some of us, this happens more often than we would care to admit! For example, how often do we think "I don't get it" when someone tells a joke, makes a pun, or inserts a comment based on a double-entendre? As adults, we can generally find other ways to figure out ambiguous material. We use contextual cues, look in a dictionary, or ask a friend. Although children of 8 or 9 years of age are presumed to be cognitively ready to understand much of the ambiguous language they encounter, the development of metalinguistic skills needed to detect ambiguity and deal with figurative language continues until 13 or 14 years of age (Hakes, 1982; Nippold, 1985; van Kleeck, 1984; Wallach and Miller, 1988). In fact, Nippold (1988) and Spector (1990), in comparing adolescents with language-learning disorders with adolescents who have normal language development, found that even the normally developing adolescents did not completely understand abstract, figurative language. It is probable that the ability to understand and appreciate the subtleties of ambiguous language continues to develop into and throughout adulthood.

Not understanding ambiguous words, phrases, or sentences in books can impair literacy, and to admit that we don't understand what is being said can be embarrassing or make us feel foolish. Not understanding ambiguity, in general, can cause a loss of the pleasure given by the many forms of humor and wordplay based on linguistic ambiguity.

INDIVIDUALS WITH LANGUAGE-LEARNING DISORDERS

The language used for academic purposes differs significantly from conversational language. In the give-and-take of conversations, there are opportunities to clarify meaning. Immediate feedback from a conversational partner makes it possible to revise utterances when misinterpretations occur, and contextual cues (such as facial expressions, gestures, body language, and tone of voice) in conversational interactions lend further support for appropriate interpretation. Given that academic language frequently does not offer this type of support, many individuals with language-learning disorders (LLD) have considerable difficulty in their academic pursuits, particularly in language arts and English. Understanding the abstract elements of language can be difficult in conversational language. It is especially difficult in a learning situation. Skill in understanding multiple meaning words and phrases and ambiguous or figurative expressions is important to school achievement.

Textbooks contain a considerable amount of nonliteral language, and, after approximately fourth grade, nonliteral language (such as idioms, analogies, indirect and polite requests, and sarcasm) frequently is found in "teacher talk" as well as in conversational speech (Hoffman and Honeck, 1980; Nelson, 1984). In fact, two-thirds of the English language contains ambiguities (Arnold and Hornett, 1990; Boatner and Gates, 1975).

Individuals with normal language development recognize the multiple meanings of frequently used words by age eight or nine. This is the most basic and simplest form of ambiguity. In contrast, individuals with LLD may not perceive the multiple meanings of even the most frequently used words. Their understanding of abstract, figurative language, in general, is poor (Nippold, 1988; Spector, 1990; Wiig and Secord, 1989). In addition, there appears to be a strong relationship between understanding figurative or ambiguous language, reading ability, and vocabulary development (Nippold, 1988).

Some of the basic principles of cognitive learning theories often are not applied in the academic setting. Teachers are not always aware of the current level of development of individuals with LLD, and consequently, many of the classroom activities provided are too difficult and tend to overwhelm these students. Teachers do not always simplify their questions and comments to the degree needed by these individuals. Verbal interactions in academic settings may be occurring too rapidly and with too much information at any one time (Blank and Marquis, 1987).

Individuals with LLD who have difficulty grasping ambiguous language need to develop their metacognitive and metalinguistic skills (Gibbs, 1987; Nippold and Martin, 1989; Prinz, 1983; van Kleeck, 1984; Wiig, 1984; Wong, 1986). Unfortunately, educators often proceed on the assumption that inferencing, reasoning, and other "meta" skills are age appropriate when they are not.

Individuals with LLD generally need to have the steps involved in an activity clearly spelled out. They need help in developing the procedures required for problem solving. Normally achieving individuals generally attain these procedures with minimal assistance.

Serious problems can occur if an educator is not aware of the difficulty individuals with LLD have in communicating their need for clarification when they do not understand what has been said. Consequently, as time goes by, greater and greater gaps form in their knowledge base. Materials presented to this population must be commensurate with their level of understanding. Often this is not the case.

Although many of the difficulties with the literal aspects of language generally have diminished by the adolescent years, students in this age group with LLD still find nonliteral meanings hard to understand (Blue, 1981; Donahue and Bryan, 1984; Nippold, 1985; Spector, 1990; Wiig and Semel, 1984). Blue (1981) noted that individuals with LLD often take utterances containing idiomatic expressions, sarcastic remarks, ambiguous statements, and words with multiple meanings in the literal sense. Such utterances "are so much a part of the adult's verbal repertoire that the user tends to be unaware of the confusion that may result for the unsophisticated listener" (Blue, 1981, p. 120). Therefore, communication problems that persist into adolescence appear to have increasingly negative consequences (Donahue and Bryan, 1984; Larson and McKinley, 1995).

Nelson (1993) and Nippold (1991) stress that many individuals with LLD do not grasp ambiguous material on their own. They need repeated exposure, with mediation, to ensure comprehension.

INDIVIDUALS WITH HEARING IMPAIRMENT

Individuals with impaired hearing frequently miss the nuances of abstract language. According to Nelson (1993), figurative meanings are learned almost exclusively through language. Individuals with normal hearing are exposed daily to hundreds of multiple meaning words and phrases just in the process of hearing or overhearing language. Figurative language is used in natural contexts that are not intended for directly teaching language. Individuals with impaired hearing lack this input.

The negative effects of even a mild hearing loss can be considerable. A speech sound may be heard in one context but not in another, depending on the sounds that surround it. Rapid speech makes it difficult for individuals with impaired hearing to determine linguistic boundaries because important stress and intonation cues for an ambiguous word, phrase, or sentence may not be heard. For example, the expression "He fed her dog biscuits" can be interpreted as "He fed *her* dog biscuits" or "He fed her *dog* biscuits." The difference in meaning is readily apparent.

Fluctuating hearing loss may enable an individual to hear differences between sounds at one time but not at another (Friel-Patti, 1990). Minimal sound changes can be crucial to understanding. The following jokes illustrate why individuals with impaired hearing often have comprehension difficulties:

- "What time do ducks get up?" "At the *quack* of dawn."

- "Why do girl mice always beat boy mice in a race?" "Because *mice* guys always finish last."

The preceding bits of humor depend on grasping small sound differences. The only way individuals with impaired hearing would realize what is funny is if they were skilled speech readers or if the jokes were presented in written form.

Individuals with impaired hearing have even greater difficulty understanding the figurative meaning of multiple meaning words and phrases when they are embedded in unfamiliar topics. Generally, they have smaller vocabularies than individuals with normal hearing ability, restricted world experience, and difficulty with complex syntactic structures (Arnold and Hornett, 1990; Moeller, Osberger, and Eccarius, 1986; Robbins 1986). Of course, the degree to which individuals with impaired hearing will deviate from the general population in their language skills depends on the nature of their hearing loss and the age at which diagnosis and significant intervention occurs.

Although it may be difficult, individuals who are deaf or hearing impaired can understand figurative or ambiguous language when it is presented in an appropriate manner and with sufficiently frequent exposure (Iran-Nejad, Ortony, and Rittenhouse, 1981; Smith, Schloss, and Israelite, 1986). The acquisition of metacognitive strategies (such as those presented in this text) has been shown to improve thinking proficiency related to problem solving and abstract language in individuals with impaired hearing (Haywood, Towery-Woolsey, Arbitman-Smith, and Aldridge, 1988).

INDIVIDUALS WITH BRAIN INJURY

Approximately 400,000 traumatic brain injuries (TBIs) occur each year in the United States. As a result, 30,000 to 50,000 individuals are left with severe physical, cognitive, or psychosocial disabilities (Kalsbeek, McLaurin, Harris, and Miller, 1980). The highest risk group for TBI includes active adolescents and young adults in the 15- to 25-year age range (Ylvisaker, Kolpan, and Rosenthal, 1994). TBI may result from closed or open head trauma. Open head injuries are caused by missiles (for example, bullets) or other objects that penetrate the skull. Closed head injuries, typically associated with motor vehicle or bicycle accidents, falls, sports accidents, and assault, are injuries in which a blunt blow to the head can cause a wide range of brain lesions. These lesions may seriously damage brain functioning.

Individuals with severe closed head injuries characteristically evidence many pervasive neurobehavioral deficits. Among these are ineffective problem solving and generally ineffective control over cognitive and communicative behavior. More specifically, there is difficulty in the following areas: using contextual cues to help interpret language, understanding abstract language, grasping implied meaning, processing ambiguity or shifting from one meaning to another, and following rapidly spoken language. These difficulties occur in verbal exchanges as well as in viewing pictures and ongoing events (Myers, 1986).

After they recover basic communication skills, many TBI patients appear to return to pretraumatic levels of functioning. However, close inspection may reveal subtle deficits in abstract, higher level cognitive skills (Haarbauer-Krupa, Henry, Szekeres, and Ylvisaker, 1985). Often there is reduced understanding of abstractness in others' language (such as ambiguity, satire, and drawing inferences). These individuals have to be taught how to figure out the meaning of idioms and other ambiguous words and phrases (Blosser and DePompei, 1989).

Another consideration is the level of the individual's pretrauma metalinguistic skills. It is possible that ambiguous language may have been problematic even before TBI was incurred. Dealing with nonliteral or ambiguous language may be more difficult if the deficits are developmental as well as trauma induced. Family members, if available, may offer insights into pretraumatic levels of functioning.

Generally, the left hemisphere of the brain is considered dominant in controlling language, whether verbal or written, and is particularly sensitive to temporal ordering. Damage to this hemisphere would affect sequential processing. This type of processing is involved in providing information necessary to achieve linguistic insights and enables us to reflect upon the contents of information (McGhee, 1983). However, individuals who have sustained damage in either hemisphere of the brain are likely to have difficulty with ambiguous language. The effects of right cerebral hemisphere damage on communicative capacity cannot be underestimated (Myers and Mackisack, 1990). Simultaneous processing, associated primarily with the right hemisphere, also is crucial to achieving linguistic insights. It is how key elements of information are linked meaningfully. Individuals who have right hemisphere lesions show "reduced ability to:

1. consider connotations of words
2. interpret simple metaphors
3. organize information into coherent sequences
4. detect bizarre or incongruous elements
5. integrate details into a broader coherent whole
6. judge plausibility of an event relative to a particular context
7. consider interrelationships between parts
8. go beyond specific details to 'get the point' of a message" (McGhee, 1983, p. 30).

Thus, appreciation of sophisticated language (such as humor based on ambiguity) requires that an individual be capable of holistic cognitive processing.

INDIVIDUALS FROM CULTURALLY AND LINGUISTICALLY DIVERSE GROUPS

INDIVIDUALS LEARNING ENGLISH AS A SECOND LANGUAGE

Individuals learning English as a second language (ESL), given sufficient time, generally master the more concrete aspects of morphology, phonology, and syntax. They learn how words are formed from sounds and how parts of words change meaning (for example, adding *s* to make a word plural or *ed* to change tense). They have knowledge of speech sounds and the rules for sequencing and using these sounds (for example, *ng* is not found at the beginning of English words, but can be found in the middle [di*ng*y, hu*ng*ry] or end of words [goi*ng*, bei*ng*]), and they understand the rules specifying word order, sentence organization, and word relationships. However, individuals who are learning English as a second language have great difficulty understanding ambiguous material. The ambiguous elements of the English language, such as words with multiple meanings or idiomatic expressions, are elusive. Idioms, metaphors, and proverbs are difficult because their meanings are ambiguous and have to be inferred through knowledge of the context. Attempts to look up the words comprising a figurative expression in a dictionary (unless it is an idiom dictionary) will generally prove to be confusing because the meaning of the expression is different from the sum of the meanings of the individual words. Humor, which often is based on ambiguity, is probably one of the last aspects of culture that a second language learner understands (Cheng, 1996).

Although basic interpersonal (peer appropriate) communication skills are achieved within two to three years, it takes from *five to seven years* for ESL students to achieve English proficiency for cognitive academic tasks (Cummins, 1989). Since, as previously mentioned, two-thirds of the English language contains ambiguities, poor understanding of ambiguous language would have a serious impact on academic and social-personal interactions (Boyce and Larson, 1983; Donahue and Bryan, 1984; Spector, 1990; Wiig, 1984).

Also to be considered is whether an individual learning English as a second language has developed the metalinguistic skills necessary for understanding ambiguities in his or her primary language. If an individual does have these skills, then it is just a matter of providing a sufficient amount of structured exposure to the ambiguities in the English language. If not, exposure plus the development of metalinguistic skills will be necessary.

Spector (1994) studied high school students, ranging in age from 15 to 20 years, who were in ESL classes. No significant differences in understanding ambiguities (based on multiple meaning words, idiomatic expressions, changes in stress, or multiple meaning sentences) were found between students who were in the United States for one, two, three, or four years. Her results indicate that casual exposure to ambiguous language is not sufficient for these students to grasp its meaning. For example, they were asked to interpret the idiom *working for peanuts* in this joke:

Question: "Why did Snoopy want to quit the comic strip?"

Answer: "He was tired of working for Peanuts."

The following responses were given:

- Literal interpretations: "No salary, no money. You work and you get peanuts back"; "They were paying him with peanuts."

- Tangential or unrelated interpretations: "He was sick of it, he was getting bored"; "When you don't want to work anymore"; "Working for stupid people. He was tired of working for them."

- Related interpretations: "The job is not good, not important."

Only a few of the students showed understanding that the expression means an individual is working for very little pay by giving responses such as "Working without getting much money or benefits," "Working for a low salary," or "Low wage."

COUNTRY-OF-ORIGIN INFLUENCES

Individuals from Asian countries use specific language forms to address others with respect to their age and social status (Owens, 1992). Indeed, social status is an important issue in general for this population, and it appeared to be a factor for a Vietnamese student in her interpretation of the idiom *working for peanuts* ("This job is not good, not important").

Some figurative expressions are common to two (or more) languages but vary in interpretation, depending on the country where the expression is used. For example, a member of my family (an American) studied in France. His class at the university was asked to interpret the proverb "A rolling stone gathers no moss" ("Pierre qui roule n'amasse pas mousse"). The American students in the group gave the following interpretations: "If you keep moving, you will stay physically fit"; "Be ambitious. Don't sit around if you want to get ahead in life"; "If you don't keep moving you will miss out on life's adventures and challenges"; "If you keep moving around, you won't have possessions or responsibilities." The French students, on the other hand, offered interpretations that can be summed up as meaning that it's a good idea for one to stay put so roots can be established. Only the last of the American students' interpretations resembles the French version. How we interpret what we hear appears to be influenced by the social and cultural values of our country of origin.

CONFUSION CAUSED BY VISUAL CUES

Body language, eye contact, or gestures in one country may have a different meaning in another. For example, individuals from Spanish-speaking countries use indirect eye contact as a sign of respect, and children from Asian countries generally avert their eyes to be polite when talking with adults. Speakers of African American English (AAE) also consider averting one's eyes a sign of politeness when listening to a conversational partner (Owens, 1992). If, for example, a character in a cartoon or a comic strip casts his eyes down as he listens to another character, individuals who are from the United States and use Standard American English (SAE) would consider this an indication that the character is shy, embarrassed, or possibly rude. Individuals from Asian or Spanish-speaking countries or those who use AAE would probably consider the lowering of the gaze as an indication of politeness and respect. The possibility of differing interpretations of the same visual material may lead individuals from other cultural backgrounds to draw erroneous conclusions about the intent or meaning of a cartoon, comic strip, or advertisement.

MORPHOLOGICAL AND PHONOLOGICAL DIFFERENCES BETWEEN LANGUAGES

Butler (1996) cites a study by Donato and Hernandez (1993) who found, in their review of recent research, that bilingual students have greater skill than monolinguals to reflect upon and analyze the language they use. Even so, dealing with the switch from one phonological (or morphological) system to another can be problematic. For example, the omission, weakening, or substitution of final consonants is a characteristic of African-Americans. The English of Hispanic and Arabic speakers often is characterized by the elimination of the plural /s/, while the English of Asian language speakers is characterized by elimination of final consonant clusters (Cheng, 1996; Wilson, 1996). Consider the difficulty encountered in interpreting the following joke, which depends on recognizing the significance of a grammatical marker often omitted by the aforementioned populations:

"What did Snow White sing while waiting for her photos?"

"Someday my *prints* will come."

Many ESL speakers tend to shorten, lengthen, or change vowels depending upon their original dialect. In Arabic English, for example, *bit* becomes *bet*, and *hope* becomes *hop*. The meaning of words in which such vowels are found can become obscure or ambiguous. Arabic speakers of English also differ in their use of linguistic stress. Stress is predictable in Arabic, but not in English. These speakers have difficulty grasping the changes in stress that can alter meaning (Wilson, 1996). This could create problems when ambiguities based on stress and juncture changes are encountered. The word *content*, for example, is a noun when the first syllable is stressed, '*con tent* (substance, essential meaning), and a verb when the second syllable is stressed *con* '*tent* (happy, satisfied). Or consider how the intent or meaning of the following response changes when different words are stressed:

"Who gave her the bell?" "*She* gave her the bell."

"To whom did she give the bell?" "She gave *her* the bell."

"What did she give her?" "She gave her the *bell*."

Even gestures may take on a different meaning from one culture to another. Holding up one's hand and making a circle with the thumb and index finger, for example, is a positive sign of praise to speakers of American English, but is a negative, derogatory sign in Brazil. Therefore, we cannot assume that verbal and nonverbal cues and visual details (in cartoons and comic strips) pertaining to facial expression, body posture, and an individual's status will be interpreted in the manner expected by Americans who use English as their primary language.

Materials developed for ESL students generally have contrived exercises that do not provide adequate contextual support (Irujo, 1986). Irujo recommended the use of logical, supportive contexts for expanding an ESL learner's knowledge of ambiguous language. The Institute for Educational Research (1990) suggested that ESL students engage in tasks that require higher level thinking to encourage development of metalinguistic skills. Understanding ambiguous language presents just such a challenge. Bilingual students, or those who speak nonstandard dialects of American English, would be likely to benefit from formal instruction in ambiguous language, especially idioms, since they do not translate easily from one language to another and often are specific to certain cultural groups or geographic locations (Nippold and Martin, 1989).

APPENDIX B

THE INFLUENCE OF COGNITIVE LEARNING THEORIES

Cognitive learning theories have influenced the cognitive strategy approach implemented in *Saying One Thing, Meaning Another*. Cognitive learning theories focus on internal aspects of behavior and the individual's regulation of learning (Carrow-Woolfolk, 1988; Nelson, 1993; van Kleeck and Richardson, 1986). There are theories that explain *what* needs to be learned and theories that focus on *how* learning takes place. At times, it is difficult to ascertain which theory researchers are discussing because they may use different names to describe learning theories based upon a common foundation. Theories based on Vygotsky's work, for example, have been called *cognitive organization theory* by Carrow-Woolfolk (1988) and *social learning theory* by van Kleeck and Richardson (1986). Nelson (1993) categorizes these theories as *cognitivism* and *social interactivism*. Klein and Moses (1994) organized cognitive learning theories into two categories they call *constructivist-cognitive* and *social-cognitive*, based on the theorists' differing explanations of how language behaviors are acquired. For the purpose of this discussion, the Klein and Moses terminology will be used.

CONSTRUCTIVIST-COGNITIVE LEARNING THEORIES

Supporters of constructivist-cognitive learning theories propose that the developmental aspects of language are not learned directly from others but are modified as individuals interact with the environment in creative ways (Case, 1985; Fischer and Pipp, 1984; Karmiloff-Smith, 1979; Piaget, 1985; Pinker, 1991). Children's use of feedback from their own actions in the process of problem solving reflects on the development of meaning. Thinking about their own language behavior makes children aware of these behaviors (Piaget, 1985). This awareness has been called *metalinguistic knowledge* (Kamhi, 1987; Karmiloff-Smith, 1979; Pinker, 1990; van Kleeck, 1984). Basically, at the core of a constructivist-cognitive view of language development is the individual's own creative activities.

From the constructivist-cognitive viewpoint, the focus is on developmental aspects of language, where abilities are acquired in a set order and where certain abilities have to be acquired before others can emerge (Bloom and Lahey, 1978). Children engage in constructivist activities such as developing problem-solving procedures, reflecting upon actions and events in the environment, making inferences, and judging one's success or failure in achieving a language goal. Language emerges as a result of the child's constructive activity. However, it is the adult who creates a developmentally appropriate environment that allows for and stimulates constructive activity, helps to facilitate problem identification, and promotes the drawing of inferences.

Proponents of constructivist-cognitive theories believe that language learning is facilitated by the following:

- interacting with materials and tasks commensurate with the individual's past experience and present developmental level and interests;
- varying actions during problem solving;
- reflecting upon personal behavior and the environment;
- making inferences; and
- using inductive and deductive reasoning.

SOCIAL-COGNITIVE LEARNING THEORIES

The social-cognitive theories attempt to provide an explanation of how individuals learn language by focusing on their information-processing skills, how they acquire internal control over learning and problem solving, or how they learn how to learn (Reid, 1988; van Kleeck and Richardson, 1986, Vygotsky, 1962). Pragmatic skills, the learning of cultural rules for using language efficiently in various social contexts, also are examined. Social-cognitive learning theories differ from constructivist-cognitive theories in that children's development is mediated by adults. Children acquire the features of language that are modeled by the adults in their lives (for example, internalizing verbal directions or imitating problem-solving procedures). This learning also can be derived from children's peers as they interact at play or participate in problem-solving activities (Nelson, 1993). In essence, children observe, imitate, and internalize problem-solving procedures and other learning strategies demonstrated by others. They learn to use language internally to direct problem-solving procedures and to stop and redirect behavior. The adult directs the learner's attention to relevant stimuli in the environment.

Metacognition is the voluntary, selective attention to one's own cognitive processes. The social-cognitive learning theories focus upon metacognitive strategies for processing information. This involves strategies such as those needed for attending, organizing, remembering, inferencing, sequencing, and problem solving. The analysis and study of specific aspects of cognition as each is being performed are called *metaperception, metamemory,* and *metacommunication* or *metalinguistics* (Flavell and Wellman, 1980).

Both constructivist-cognitive and social-cognitive learning theories provide us with many guiding principles for devising procedures to improve understanding of ambiguous language. For example, efforts to convey meaning successfully by repairing miscommunication of meaning is considered by both to be a principle of language learning. In addition, both constructivist and social-cognitive theorists recognize the need to consider a child's developmental level when planning intervention procedures. This important learning principle is found in Vygotsky's

(1962) work. Vygotsky proposed that the influence of adults on language learning occurs within a *zone of proximal development.* This zone is that area between the child's developmental level as manifested in spontaneous behavior and the level the child can potentially achieve with adult guidance. Vygotsky views the child as developing and functioning within a social context. Social interaction is essential for the individual to develop. Schneider and Watkins (1996) discuss the need for ongoing interaction, which enables the individual to internalize strategies provided by the facilitator in joint problem-solving activities. The essential feature of this interaction is that facilitators be able to adjust their assistance to the needs of the individual, retaining responsibility when the individual is less successful and relinquishing it when the individual is doing well. The individual is learning the process of identifying the steps involved in an activity, not just how to perform any specific activity.

According to Lidz (1991), facilitators can mediate an experience in a dynamic interaction in the following ways:

- by helping the individual discriminate between what is important and what is not;

- by helping the individual go from other- to self-regulation;

- by mediating goal seeking, setting, and planning; and

- by mediating the level of difficulty of the activity so the individual can realize greater levels of competency without being overwhelmed.

Social theorists stress naturalistic context as a strong determining factor in the acquisition of language structures. These theorists also recognize the need for language facilitators to adapt their input in response to the current needs of the individual with whom they are interacting, and to provide environmental experiences to assist individuals in expanding their world knowledge (that is, they should use relevant content and contexts). Social theorists stress language function over language structure, as well as the importance of context.

Although the issue of assisting individuals who have lost language skills through brain injury or individuals who are learning English as a second language has not been addressed in this context, it seems reasonable that following the principles set forth in the constructivist-cognitive and social-cognitive theories would have a positive effect on their learning as well.

APPENDIX C
SUGGESTIONS FOR IEP GOALS AND OBJECTIVES

GOAL

To improve the individual's understanding and use of multiple meaning words

Objective: The individual will identify the word in a sentence that can be interpreted in two ways.

Objective: The individual will provide two meanings for an ambiguous word.

Objective: The individual will use context clues to determine word meaning.

Objective: The individual will use multiple meaning words appropriately.

Objective: The individual will match the meanings of homographs with their definitions.

Objective: The individual will provide two meanings for homographs.

Objective: The individual will match the meanings of homophones with their definitions.

Objective: The individual will provide two meanings for homophones.

GOAL

To improve the individual's understanding and use of sentences that can be taken in two ways

Objective: The individual will provide both meanings of a dual-meaning sentence.

Objective: The individual will paraphrase to show the alternate meaning of an ambiguous sentence.

Objective: The individual will clarify ambiguous sentences by determining which words are implied.

Objective: The individual will state the intended meaning of polite or indirect requests.

Objective: The individual will state the intended meaning of polite evasions.

Objective: The individual will state the intended meaning of ironic or sarcastic comments.

GOAL

To improve the individual's understanding and use of multiple meaning phrases

Objective: The individual will identify phrases that have multiple meanings.

Objective: The individual will provide two meanings for multiple meaning phrases.

Objective: The individual will recognize phrases that have only figurative meanings.

Objective: The individual will use context clues to determine the meaning of multiple meaning phrases.

Objective: The individual will use multiple meaning phrases appropriately.

GOAL

To improve the individual's understanding and use of ambiguity caused by changes in stress and/or juncture

Objective: The individual will recognize and select the word(s) in which altering the stress and/or juncture will result in a new meaning.

Objective: The individual will provide the new meaning created by altering the stress and/or juncture of a sentence.

Objective: The individual will use context clues to determine the new meaning created by altering the stress and/or juncture of a sentence.

Objective: The individual will use stress and intonation to appropriately alter the meaning of a sentence.

GOAL

To improve the individual's semantic language skills

Objective: The individual will paraphrase an ambiguous utterance to clarify its meaning.

Objective: The individual will recognize and explain linguistic context clues.

Objective: The individual will recognize and explain nonlinguistic context clues.

Objective: The individual will verbalize the steps taken in problem-solving tasks.

Objective: The individual will reason logically by verbalizing thoughts.

Objective: The individual will use inferencing skills to determine alternate meanings of ambiguous words, phrases, or sentences.

GOAL

To improve the individual's pragmatic language skills

Objective: The individual will request clarifying information when necessary.

Objective: The individual will provide appropriate revision when there is a breakdown in communication.

Objective: The individual will revise an utterance to eliminate ambiguity.

Objective: The individual will adequately explain an ambiguous utterance.

Objective: The individual will use ambiguous language appropriately.

APPENDIX D

IDIOM AND PROVERB DICTIONARIES AND THESAURUS

Chapman, R.L. (Ed.). (1986). *New dictionary of American slang.* New York: Harper and Row.

Gulland, D.M., and Hinds-Howell, D.G. (1994). *Dictionary of English idioms.* New York: Penguin Books.

Makkai, A., Boatner, M.T., and Gates, J.E. (1995). *A dictionary of American idioms.* New York: Barron's Educational Series.

Simpson, J. (1996). *The concise Oxford dictionary of proverbs.* New York: Oxford University Press.

Spears, R.A. (1994). *Essential American idioms.* Lincolnwood, IL: National Textbook Company.

Spears, R.A. (1996). *NTC's American idioms dictionary.* Lincolnwood, IL: National Textbook Company.

REFERENCES

Ackerman, B. (1982). On comprehending idioms: Do children get the picture? *Journal of Experimental Psychology, 33*, 439–454.

Arnold, K., and Hornett, D. (1990). Teaching idioms to children who are deaf. *Teaching Exceptional Children, 22*(4), 14–17.

Berlin, L.J., Blank, M., and Rose, S.A. (1980). The language of instruction: The hidden complexities. *Topics in Language Disorders, 1*(1), 47–58.

Blank, M., and Marquis, A. (1987). *Teaching discourse.* Tucson, AZ: Communication Skill Builders.

Bloom, L., and Lahey, M. (1978). *Language development and language disorders.* New York: John Wiley.

Blosser, J., and DePompei, R. (1989). The head-injured student returns to school: Recognizing and treating deficits. *Topics in Language Disorders, 9*(2), 67–77.

Blue, C. (1981). Types of utterances to avoid when speaking to language delayed children. *Language, Speech, and Hearing Services in Schools, 12*, 120–124.

Boatner, M., and Gates, J. (1975). *A dictionary of American idioms.* Woodbury, NY: Barron's Educational Series.

Boyce, N., and Larson, V.L. (1983). *Adolescents' communication: Development and disorders.* Eau Claire, WI: Thinking Publications.

Brown, G., Anderson, A., Shillcock, R., and Yule, G. (1984). *Teaching talk.* New York: Cambridge University Press.

Brubaker, S. (1983). *Workbook for reasoning skills.* Detroit, MI: Wayne State University Press.

Bunce, B. (1989). Using a barrier game format to improve children's referential communication skills. *Journal of Speech and Hearing Disorders, 54*, 33–43.

Bush, C.S. (1989). *150 Skill-building reference lists: Language remediation and expansion.* San Antonio, TX: Communication Skill Builders.

Butler, K.G. (1996). From the editor. *Topics in Language Disorders, 16*(4), iv–v.

Buttrill, J., Niizawa, J., Biemer, C., Takakashi, C., and Hearn, S. (1989). Serving the language learning disabled adolescent: A strategies-based model. *Language, Speech, and Hearing Services in Schools, 20,* 185–204.

Carrow-Woolfolk, E. (1988). *Theory, assessment and intervention in language disorders: An integrative approach.* Orlando, FL: Grune and Stratton.

Case, R. (1985). *Intellectual development: Birth to adulthood.* Orlando, FL: Academic Press.

Cheng, L. (1996). Beyond bilingualism: A quest for communicative competence. *Topics in Language Disorders, 16*(4), 9–21.

Creaghead, N., and Tattershall, S. (1991). Observation and assessment of classroom pragmatic skills. In C. Simon (Ed.), *Communication skills and classroom success: Assessment and therapy methodologies for language and learning disabled students* (pp. 106–122). Eau Claire, WI: Thinking Publications.

Cummins, J. (1989). A theoretical framework for bilingual special education. *Exceptional Children, 56*(2), 111–119.

de Bettencourt, L. (1987). Strategy training: A need for clarification. *Exceptional Children, 54*(1), 24–30.

De Feo, A., Grimm, D., and Paige, P. (1988). *Making conversation idiomatic.* Tucson, AZ: Communication Skill Builders.

Dickson, W.P. (1983). Training cognitive strategies for oral communication. In M. Pressley and J.R. Levin (Eds.), *Cognitive strategy research* (pp. 29–42). New York: Springer-Verlag.

Donahue, M., and Bryan, T. (1984). Communicative skills and peer relations of learning disabled adolescents. *Topics in Language Disorders, 4*(2), 10–21.

Donato, R., and Hernandez, J.S. (1993). Metacognitive equity for Mexican American language minority students: Questions of equity. *The Journal of Educational Issues of Language Minority Students, Special Issue III, 12,* 17–34.

Fischer, K., and Pipp, S. (1984). Processes of cognitive development: Optimal level and skill acquisition. In R. Sternberg (Ed.), *Mechanisms of cognitive development* (pp. 45–81). New York: Freeman.

Flavell, J.H., and Wellman, H.M. (1980). Metamemory. In R.V. Kail and J.W. Hagen (Eds.), *Memory in cognitive development* (pp. 3–33). Hillsdale, NJ: Erlbaum.

Friel-Patti, S. (1990). Otitis media with effusion and the development of language: A review of the evidence. *Topics in Language Disorders, 11*(1), 11–22.

Gallagher, T.M. (1991). Language and social skills: Implications for clinical assessment and intervention with school-age children. In T.M. Gallagher (Ed.), *Pragmatics of language: Clinical practice issues* (pp. 11–41). San Diego, CA: Singular.

Gelzheiser, L.M. (1984). Generalization from categorical memory tasks to prose by learning disabled adolescents. *Journal of Educational Psychology, 76,* 1126–1138.

Gibbs, R. (1986). Skating on thin ice: Literal meaning and understanding in conversation. *Discourse Processes, 9*(1), 17–30.

Gibbs, R. (1987). Linguistic factors in children's understanding of idioms. *Journal of Child Language, 14,* 569–586.

Gorman-Gard, K. (1992). *Figurative language.* Greenville, SC: Super Duper® Publications.

Haarbauer-Krupa, J., Henry, K., Szekeres, S., and Ylvisaker, M. (1985). Cognitive rehabilitation therapy: Late stages of recovery. In M. Ylvisaker (Ed.), *Head injury rehabilitation: Children and adolescents* (pp. 311–343). San Diego, CA: College-Hill.

Hakes, D. (1982). The development of metalinguistic ability: What develops? In S. Kuczaj (Ed.), *Language development: Language, thought, and culture* (Vol. 2). Hillsdale, NJ: Erlbaum.

Hamersky, J. (1995). *Cartoon cut-ups.* Greenville, SC: Super Duper® Publications.

Haywood, H.C., Towery-Woolsey, J., Arbitman-Smith, R., and Aldridge, A. (1988). Cognitive education with deaf adolescents: Effects of instrumental enrichment. *Topics in Language Disorders, 8*(4), 23–40.

Hirsch-Pasek, K., Gleitman, L.R., and Gleitman, H. (1978). What did the brain say to the mind? A study of the detection and report of ambiguity by young children. In A. Sinclair, R.J. Jarvella, and W. J.M. Levelt (Eds.), *The child's conception of language* (pp. 97–132). Berlin: Springer-Verlag.

Hoffman, R.R., and Honeck, R.P. (1980). A peacock looks at its legs: Cognitive science and figurative language. In R.P. Honeck and R.R. Hoffman (Eds.), *Cognition and figurative language* (pp. 3–24). Hillsdale, NJ: Erlbaum.

Honeck, R.P., Sowry, B.M., and Voegtle, K. (1978). Proverbial understanding in a pictorial context. *Child Development, 49,* 327–331.

Huisingh, R., Barrett, M., Zachman, L., Blagden, C., and Orman, J. (1990). *The word test–revised.* East Moline, IL: LinguiSystems.

Institute for Educational Research. (1990). Accommodating diversity. *American Teacher, 8*(74), 2.

Iran-Nejad, A., Ortony, A., and Rittenhouse, R. (1981). The comprehension of metaphorical uses of English by deaf children. *Journal of Speech and Hearing Research, 24,* 551–556.

Irujo, S. (1986). A piece of cake: Learning and teaching idioms. *English Language Teaching Journal, 40,* 236–242.

Kalsbeek, W.D., McLaurin, R.L., Harris, B.S.H., and Miller, J.D. (1980). The national head and spinal cord injury survey: Major findings. *Journal of Neurosurgery, 53*(Suppl.), 19–31.

Kamhi, A.G. (1987). Metalinguistic abilities in language-impaired children. *Topics in Language Disorders, 7*(2), 1–12.

Kamhi, A.G., Lee, R., and Nelson, L. (1985). Word, syllable, and sound awareness in language-disordered children. *Journal of Speech and Hearing Disorders, 50,* 207–212.

Karmiloff-Smith, A. (1979). *A functional approach to child language.* Cambridge, UK: Cambridge University Press.

Klein, H.B., and Moses, N. (1994). *Intervention planning for children with communication disorders.* Englewood Cliffs, NJ: Prentice Hall.

Lahey, M. (1988). *Language disorders and language development.* New York: Macmillan.

Larson, V. Lord, and McKinley, N. (1987). *Communication assessment and intervention strategies for adolescents.* Eau Claire, WI: Thinking Publications.

Larson, V. Lord, and McKinley, N. (1995). *Language disorders in older students: Preadolescents and adolescents.* Eau Claire, WI: Thinking Publications.

Lazar, R., Warr-Leeper, G., Beel-Nicholson, C., and Johnson, S. (1989). Elementary school teachers' use of multiple meaning expressions. *Language, Speech, and Hearing Services in Schools, 20,* 420–430.

Lee, R., and Kamhi, A. (1985, November). *Verbal metaphor performance in learning disabled children.* Paper presented at the annual convention of the American Speech-Language-Hearing Association, Washington, DC.

Lidz, C.S. (1991). *Practitioner's guide to dynamic assessment.* New York: Guilford.

Lloyd, P. (1994). Referential communication: Assessment and intervention. *Topics in Language Disorders, 14*(3), 55–69.

McGhee, P.E. (1983). The role of arousal and hemispheric lateralization in humor. In P.E. McGhee and J.H. Goldstein (Eds.), *Handbook of humor research* (pp. 13–37). New York: Springer-Verlag.

McKinley, N., and Larson, V.L. (1985). Neglected language disordered adolescents: A delivery model. *Language, Speech, and Hearing Services in Schools, 16,* 2–15.

Milosky, L.M. (1990). The role of world knowledge in language comprehension and language intervention. *Topics in Language Disorders, 10*(3), 1–13.

Milosky, L.M., and Ford, J.A. (1993, April). *Variables affecting figurative language performance: Assessment and intervention applications.* Miniseminar presented at the annual convention of the New York State Speech-Language-Hearing Association, Syracuse, NY.

Moeller, M.P., Osberger, M.J., and Eccarius, M. (1986). Cognitively based strategies for use with hearing-impaired students with comprehension deficits. *Topics in Language Disorders, 6*(4), 37–50.

Myers, P.S. (1986). Right hemisphere communication impairment. In R. Chapey (Ed.), *Language intervention strategies in adult aphasia* (pp. 444–461). Baltimore: Williams and Wilkins.

Myers, P.S., and Mackisack, E.L. (1990). Right hemisphere syndrome. In L.L. LaPointe (Ed.), *Aphasia and related neurogenic language disorders* (pp. 177–195). NY: Thieme Medical.

Nelson, N.W. (1984). Beyond information processing: The language of teachers and textbooks. In G.P. Wallach and K.G. Butler (Eds.), *Language learning disabilities in school-age children* (pp. 154–178). Baltimore: Williams and Wilkins.

Nelson, N.W. (1987). *Planning individualized speech and language intervention programs: Objectives for infants, children, and adolescents.* Tucson, AZ: Communication Skill Builders.

Nelson, N.W. (1988). The nature of literacy. In M.A. Nippold (Ed.), *Later language development: Ages nine to nineteen* (pp. 11–28). Boston: Little, Brown and Company.

Nelson, N.W. (1993). *Childhood language disorders in context: Infancy through adolescence.* New York: Macmillan.

Nippold, M.A. (1985). Comprehension of figurative language in youth. *Topics in Language Disorders, 5*(3), 1–20.

Nippold, M.A. (1988). Linguistic ambiguity. In M.A. Nippold (Ed.), *Later language development: Ages nine through nineteen* (pp. 211–223). Boston: College-Hill.

Nippold, M.A. (1991). Evaluating and enhancing idiom comprehension in language disordered students. *Language, Speech, and Hearing Services in Schools, 22,* 100–106.

Nippold, M.A., and Fey, S.H. (1983). Metaphoric understanding in preadolescents having a history of language acquisition difficulties. *Language, Speech, and Hearing Services in Schools, 14,* 171–180.

Nippold, M.A., and Martin, S.T. (1989). Idiom interpretation in isolation versus context: A developmental study with adolescents. *Journal of Speech and Hearing Research, 32,* 59–66.

Nippold, M.A., Martin, S.T., and Erskine, B. (1988). Proverb comprehension in context: A developmental study with children and adolescents. *Journal of Speech and Hearing Research, 31,* 19–28.

Nippold, M.A., and Rudzinski, M. (1993). Familiarity and transparency in idiom explanations: A developmental study of children and adolescents. *Journal of Speech and Hearing Research, 36,* 728–737.

Nippold, M.A., Uhden, L.D., and Schwarz, I.E. (1997). Proverb explanation through the lifespan: A developmental study of adolescents and adults. *Journal of Speech, Language, and Hearing Research, 40,* 245–253.

Owens, R.E. (1992). *Language development: An introduction.* New York: Macmillan.

Pehrsson, R.S., and Denner, P.R. (1988). Semantic organizers: Implications for reading and writing. *Topics in Language Disorders, 8*(3), 24–37.

Pellegrini, A., and Galda, L. (1982). The effect of thematic-fantasy play training on the development of children's story comprehension. *American Educational Research Journal, 19,* 443–452.

Pflaum, S.W., and Pascarella, E.T. (1980). Interactive effects of prior reading achievement and training in context on the reading of learning disabled children. *Reading Research Quarterly, 16,* 138–158.

Piaget, J. (1985). *The equilibration of cognitive structures.* Chicago: University of Chicago Press.

Pinker, S. (1990). Language acquisition. In D.N. Osherson and H. Lasnik (Eds.), *An invitation to cognitive science* (pp. 197–241). Cambridge, MA: Massachusetts Institute of Technology Press.

Pinker, S. (1991). *Learnability and cognition.* Cambridge, MA: Massachusetts Institute of Technology Press.

Prinz, P. (1983). The development of idiomatic meaning in children. *Language and Speech, 26,* 263–272.

Prutting, C.A., and Kirchner, D.M. (1987). A clinical appraisal of the pragmatic aspects of language. *Journal of Speech and Hearing Disorders, 52,* 105–119.

Reid, D.K. (1988). *Teaching the learning disabled: A cognitive developmental approach.* Needham, MA: Allyn and Bacon.

Robbins, A.M. (1986). Facilitating language comprehension in young hearing-impaired children. *Topics in Language Disorders, 6*(3), 12–24.

Schneider, P., and Watkins, R.V. (1996). Applying Vygotskian developmental theory to language intervention. *Language, Speech, and Hearing Services in Schools, 27*(2), 157–170.

Schumaker, J.B., Deshler, D.D., Alley, G.R., and Warner, M.M. (1983). Toward the development of an intervention model for learning disabled adolescents. *Exceptional Education Quarterly, 4,* 45–74.

Schumaker, J.B., Deshler, D.D., Alley, G.R., Warner, M.M., and Denton, P. (1984). Multipass. A learning strategy for improving reading comprehension. *Learning Disability Quarterly, 5,* 295–304.

Seidenberg, P.L. (1988). Cognitive and academic instructional intervention for learning-disabled adolescents. *Topics in Language Disorders, 8*(3), 56–71.

Smith, M., Schloss, P., and Israelite, N. (1986). Evaluation of a simile recognition treatment program for hearing impaired students. *Journal of Speech and Hearing Disorders, 51,* 134–139.

Spector, C.C. (1990). Linguistic humor comprehension of normal and language-impaired adolescents. *Journal of Speech and Hearing Disorders, 55,* 533–541.

Spector, C.C. (1992). Remediating humor comprehension deficits in language-impaired students. *Language, Speech, and Hearing Services in Schools, 23,* 20–27.

Spector, C.C. (1993). *Just for laughs.* San Antonio, TX: Communication Skill Builders.

Spector, C.C. (1994, November). *ESL students' comprehension of idioms in humor.* Poster session presented at the annual convention of the American Speech-Language-Hearing Association, New Orleans, LA.

Spector, C.C. (1996). Children's comprehension of idioms in the context of humor. *Language, Speech, and Hearing Services in Schools, 27*(4), 307–313.

Sternberg, R.J., Okagaki, L., and Jackson, A.S. (1990). Practical intelligence for success in school. *Educational Leadership, 48*(1), 35–39.

Swiecki, M., and Marston, B. (1991). *In plain English.* East Moline, IL: LinguiSystems.

Terrell, S.L. (1996). Discrepancy model: Questions of concern regarding use for culturally different children. *Special Interest Divisions Newsletter, Asha, 3*(1), 8–9.

Thorum, A.R. (1986). *The Fullerton language test for adolescents* (2nd ed.) Palo Alto, CA: Consulting Psychologists Press.

van Kleeck, A. (1984). Metalinguistic skills: Cutting across spoken and written language and problem-solving abilities. In G. Wallach and K. Butler (Eds.), *Language learning disabilities in school-age children* (pp. 128–153). Baltimore: Williams and Wilkins.

van Kleeck, A. (1987). The metas: Implications for the language impaired. *Topics in Language Disorders, 7*(2), vi–vii.

van Kleeck, A., and Richardson, A. (1986). What's in an error? Wrong responses as language teaching opportunities. *NSSLHA Journal, 14,* 25–50.

Vygotsky, L.S. (1962). *Thought and language.* Cambridge, MA: Massachusetts Institute of Technology Press.

Wallach, G.P., and Lee, D.A. (1980). So you want to know what to do with language disabled children above the age of six. *Topics in Language Disorders, 1,* 99–113.

Wallach, G.P., and Miller, L. (1988). *Language intervention and academic* success. Boston: College-Hill.

Watson, R. (1985). Towards a theory of definition. *Journal of Child Language, 12,* 181–197.

Wiig, E.H. (1984). Language disabilities in adolescents: A question of cognitive strategies. *Topics in Language Disorders, 4*(2), 41–58.

Wiig, E.H. (1985). *Words, expressions, contexts.* Austin, TX: Psychological Corporation.

Wiig, E.H., and Secord, W.A. (1989). *Test of language competence–expanded edition (TLC–E).* San Antonio, TX: Psychological Corporation.

Wiig, E.H., and Secord, W.A. (1992). *Test of word knowledge.* Austin, TX: Psychological Corporation.

Wiig, E.H., and Semel, E.M. (1984). *Language assessment and intervention for the learning disabled.* Columbus, OH: Merrill.

Wilson, M.E. (1996). Arabic speakers: Language and culture, here and abroad. *Topics in Language Disorders, 16*(4), 65–80.

Winner, E., Engel, M., and Gardner, H. (1980). Misunderstanding metaphor: What's the problem? *Journal of Experimental Child Psychology, 30,* 22–32.

Wong, B.Y.L. (1986). Metacognition and special education: A review of a view. *The Journal of Special Education, 20*(1), 9–29.

Wong, B.Y.L., and Jones, W. (1982). Increasing metacomprehension in learning disabled and normally achieving students through self-questioning training. *Learning Disability Quarterly, 5,* 228–246.

Ylvisaker, M., Kolpan, K.I., and Rosenthal, M. (1994). Collaboration in preparing for personal injury suits after TBI. *Topics in Language Disorders, 15*(1), 1–18.

Ylvisaker, M., and Szekeres, S.F. (1989). Metacognitive and executive impairments in head-injured children and adults. *Topics in Language Disorders, 9*(2), 34–49.